I0499901

Options Trading Strategies

Advanced Guide with All the Latest Winning Strategies, Practical Tips, and Suggestions That Will Make the Difference in Your Trading. Start Generating Income Now

Brian Johnson

© Copyright 2019 by Brian Johnson - All rights reserved.

This eBook is provided with the sole purpose of providing relevant information on a specific topic for which every reasonable effort has been made to ensure that it is both accurate and reasonable. Nevertheless, by purchasing this eBook you consent to the fact that the author, as well as the publisher, are in no way experts on the topics contained herein, regardless of any claims as such that may be made within. As such, any suggestions or recommendations that are made within are done so purely for entertainment value. It is recommended that you always consult a professional prior to undertaking any of the advice or techniques discussed within.

This is a legally binding declaration that is considered both valid and fair by both the Committee of Publishers Association and the American Bar Association and should be considered as legally binding within the United States.

The reproduction, transmission, and duplication of any of the content found herein, including any specific or extended information will be done as an illegal act regardless of the end form the information ultimately takes. This includes copied versions of the work both physical, digital and audio unless express consent of the Publisher is provided beforehand. Any additional rights reserved.

Furthermore, the information that can be found within the pages described forthwith shall be considered both accurate and truthful when it comes to the recounting of facts. As such, any use, correct or incorrect, of the provided information will render the Publisher free of responsibility as to the actions taken outside of their direct purview. Regardless, there are zero scenarios where the original author or the Publisher can be deemed liable in any fashion for any damages or hardships that may result from any of the information discussed herein.

Additionally, the information in the following pages is intended only for informational purposes and should thus be thought of as universal. As befitting its nature, it is presented without assurance regarding its prolonged validity or interim quality. Trademarks that are mentioned are done without written consent and can in no way be considered an endorsement from the trademark holder.

Table of Contents

Introduction

Congratulations on purchasing *Options Trading Strategies: Advanced Guide with All the Latest Winning Strategies, Practical Tips, and Suggestions That Will Make the Difference in Your Trading. Start Generating Income Now,* and thank you for doing so. Most traders keep off options trading in the fear that options are too complicated or that they present too many risks, but I am glad you chose this path. Yes, options' trading is relatively complicated, but as you get more acquainted with the terms, strategies, techniques, and positions of trading, you will see that it is worth the hustle.

There is a lot of misinformation and myths surrounding options trading. Some perceive options trading to be as demanding as other investment crafts like day trading. The fact that options often come with an attached expiry date also puts many off. They are afraid that they might not sell their options in time. Others feel that options do not have many returns to offer, presuming other trades to have more returns. However, all these beliefs and many others are born out of fear and incorrect information.

The truth is that no market can exist without sellers and buyers. Just as there are sellers and buyers in other investment types, there are writers and buyers of options in the options market.

You do not have to worry about what will be bought and what won't. An expiry date doesn't necessitate immediate execution either; some may require execution, and for others, traders will just release to expire. When it comes to options trading, there is not much to worry about, and with a book as resourceful as this one, you will be well on your way to making tidy returns.

The following chapters will discuss options and options trading in depth. You will learn what options are, the types of options they are, and how traders make money. You will also get to know about brokers and the role they play, and we'll guide you on how to find one that will accommodate your investment needs. This book also lets you in on the secrets of success in options trading, and point you to some case studies that will prove to you the effectiveness of options trading over other investment methods.

There are abundant books on this topic on the market, thanks a lot yet again for picking this one! Every effort was made to guarantee it is full of as much useful material as possible. Please enjoy!

Chapter 1: Introduction to Options Trading

Calls, puts, derivatives, premiums, the strike price - the entire jargon options trading a rather complicated investment option. It doesn't compare to other investment forms like real estate or buying stocks, which are almost common knowledge. For this reason, many people do not like to get involved. However, although there is much to learn before you can dip your feet, and a lot of effort needed too, options trading may end up being one of the most rewarding investment decisions for you, in the end.

Well, the fact that there is much to learn does not mean that it is difficult; there is just a lot for you to grasp and keep in mind.

However, once you gain an understanding of the basic concepts involved, such as what options contracts are, and how options trading is conducted, the more complex issues will be very easy for you to understand. Without further delay, let's now get into the basics so that we can get you market-ready, already enjoying the proceeds of your trade.

What Are Options?

An option is a contract to buy or sell the stock at a pre-negotiated price, within a select window or before a particular date. Usually, each contract holds 100 shares of stock.

Options take the nature of investment where people buy low and sell high. You would buy a stock if you determined that the price of the stock would go up, and sell the stock if you determined that the price would go down. With an option, you would not be buying the actual asset but would be betting on the direction that the stock is likely to take.

Although options follow other assets, they are an asset in their own right. Options are one of the derivatives, the kind that derives their value from other underlying instruments. The asset from which they derive value is called underlying security or an underlying asset. As such, an option is just a contract that follows future transactions of the underlying asset.

Each option contract must indicate particular details concerning the future transaction on which the contract is based. It indicates what the prospective transaction will be, the underlying asset, the price, whether it will be sold or purchased, and the point in time by which it will be transacted.

Whenever you purchase an options contract, you are allowed, though not obliged, to do several things. First, you get the opportunity to buy or sell shares of a stock at the agreed-upon price within a limited period. Second, you get the right to sell the contract to another investor. Third, you have the option of allowing your contract to expire and then walk away without any financial obligations to any party.

So far, options may appear to be short-term investment custom-made for people who fear commitment and are only looking to capitalize on the short-term price movements by going in and out of contracts. However, that isn't the best way with which to take on options trading. Options are best suited for investors looking to make long-term investments.

Types of Options

There are two types of options from which you can choose. They are:

Put Options

Put options are premiums paid to hedge against the risk of a possible market downturn. They are similar to an insurance policy, but for your investment. With a put option, if the price of your stock falls, you will still have the privilege to sell the shares at the exercise price. However, if the market swings upward or remains stagnant, and you decide not to sell, you will only lose the premium you paid when you purchased the contract.

Call Options

A call option is a deposit right to purchase a stock at a preset date in the upcoming future. In case the call option is not exercised before the contract expires, the investor loses his or her investment and the right to purchase the stock at the strike price.

The holders of call and put options contracts are the owners of the contracts and are not obliged to sell or buy, regardless of the market performance. They are free to exercise the option whenever they see it fit.

Conversely, call and put writers are the sellers of the options contracts, and they are exposed to risks because they must follow through on their promise to sell or buy their option.

Buying or Selling Put and Call Options

In the case of trading options, you can do any of the four things. You can buy puts, sell puts, buy calls, or even sell calls.

You are in a long position at any time you buy stock. As such, when you buy a call option, you are put in a potentially long position to the underlying stock. Short-selling a stock puts you in a short position in the underlying stock, and so does selling an uncovered or naked call.

Buying a put option places you in a short position with the underlying stock. Selling uncovered or naked puts places you in a potential long position in the underlying stock.

Remember that people who sell options are called the writers of options, while those who buy options are the holders. Call and put holders, the buyers, do not have an obligation to sell or buy, but they can choose to exercise their rights. This limits their risks to the premiums they have spent.

Call and put writers and the sellers, have the obligation to sell or buy, but only when the option expires when in-the-money. This is to say that a seller has to make good of his promise to sell or buy the stock. It also means that the option seller is exposed to much more (sometimes limited) risk. As such, writers stand to lose much more than the options premium.

Why Options?

There are many reasons and benefits of using options for investment. They include:

Investing in Options Requires a Significantly Smaller Capital Outlay Compared to Purchasing the Stocks Themselves

Options are a preferred investment vehicle because they allow you to make significant profits without necessarily having to dish out large amounts of money. This makes them ideal for investors who have very little capital and for big investors with large budgets. The reason small investments produce big profits is simple; leverage gives you more trading power with the little you got, and this does not compare to the shareholder power you would have had bought stocks.

Let's consider an example. Suppose you had $4,000 to invest, and the company whose stock you wanted to buy, Company X, has its stocks currently trading at $20. You expect that the company's shares will rise in value. If you choose to purchase stocks, your $4,000 investment capital will get you just 200 shares. If the stock price increases to $25, you would make a profit of $5 for each share, which would add up to $800. You would receive a 20% return on your investment.

On the other hand, if you purchased call options on the same stock, and the call price for each share was $2, your $4,000 investment budget would allow you to acquire 2,000 options, which will have enabled you to buy 2,000 shares. If the price of the stock went up, rising to $25, you could exercise your option to buy 2,000 shares, then sell them immediately at $25, for a $10,000 income. This profit would be a 150% return on your investment.

The example above illustrates to you how you can generate sizeable returns, whichever investment level you are at. Options will give this one significant advantage over any other financial instrument. As you see, you can save quite a lot of money when you take a particular position on the underlying security because it enables you to make cost-effective trades and investments.

With Options, the Investor Is Protected from the Downsides Risk Because the Contract Locks in the Price and Does Not Place an Obligation to Buy

This benefit is called the risk versus reward advantage. As you can see in the example given above, with options, large amounts of capital and profits can be obtained from an amount that would have given less, had you invested in the actual underlying asset. This makes options a cost-efficient investment option. In addition, if the trader employs the proper trading strategies, the risks versus rewards ratio will be relatively lower.

The fact that risks are low does not mean that there are no significant risks involved; any investment type will have them. The reality is that trading strategies that are speculative, such as options, can be very risky. The general rule, however, is that the higher the potential returns, the higher the risks involved. The good thing, though, is that you have the liberty to choose the level of risk you are willing to take and then do all you can to minimize it.

Risks are also more spread out for options because there is a wide range of options contracts and different orders you can take in, which makes it easier to limit the risk you expose yourself to than it would be if you were buying and selling stock.

Options can also be a tool for limiting the exposure to risks on the stock options you have already. For example, if you already own stock for a particular company and have concerns about the short-term volatility of the stocks because it could wipe out your gains, you can hedge against these possible losses. To hedge against these losses, buy a 'put' option because it will give you the right to sell a given number of shares at a specified price. If the share price goes down, the options contract will limit your losses and the gains you will get when you sell the contract will help to offset some of the losses.

As you go further in learning about options and the way they are traded, you will see just what an incredible tool they are when it comes to managing risks.

Options Buy the Investor Time to See How the Market Plays Out.

If you have been eyeing a company and you believe that its stock price will rise, you will opt for a call option because it will give you the right to purchase shares at a predetermined price at a specific date in the future. If it happens as you had predicted, you will buy your stock for less than it would sell in the open market. If the situation doesn't play out as you had hoped, your financial losses will be limited to the price you paid for your contract.

Options Are Flexible and Adaptable

One of the biggest pros of options is the flexibility options offer. This is unlike most passive income investments and some active ones too that have limited strategies and techniques for making money.

If you were to take the conventional buy and hold approach that involves merely buying stocks and building a portfolio in the long-term, only two investment strategies would be available to you. You may choose to buy stocks that will appreciate with time and cash in on this long-term growth, or you may want to buy stocks whose companies offer regular dividend payouts, and you will enjoy the regular returns. Some people even diversify their portfolio and use a combination of the two.

When using the traditional buy and hold strategies discussed above, the investor has to choose between whether to make very safe investments that give little returns or whether to endure more risks but have the potential for large profits. That said, with only two possible strategies, there isn't much scope as to how far your advanced strategies can go. There are not many options to increase your profits, as you would have trading options.

The flexibility and versatility of options mean that there will be very many investment opportunities in spite of the market conditions prevailing. In addition, options can be traded based on a wide range of underlying assets. Also, just as you can speculate on the movement of the price of stocks, you can speculate on the movement of the price of indices, foreign currencies, and commodities. As you can see, there are a vast number of opportunities that you can turn into potential trades and reap some profits out of them.

Take, for example, a person who is good at predicting changes in the forex market also has a deep understanding of some specific industry. The individual could use his prediction skill to navigate the forex market to trade options and will use his fundamental knowledge of the particular industry to trade options based on the available stock. The potential for finding your niche in options trading is almost limitless.

The number of trading strategies from which a trader would choose is also significant. Spreads, in particular, give you the flexibility of choosing the way to trade, whether you want to limit the risk of taking up a position, want to profit from price movements in either direction, or want to reduce the upfront costs of taking up a particular position.

The spread is what allows you to have true versatility. You can use it to hedge for existing positions during times of economic uncertainty and to profit from a stagnant market. Both of these uses are impossible when trading stocks.

Disadvantages of Options

As we mentioned in the beginning, mastering all there is to do with options trading is an uphill task. There is just so much to learn and understand, and for that reason, many investors choose to avoid it. There is no straightforward path to it, and to understand what it is all about, an investor needs to invest a lot of time and commitment. However, eventually, he or she will have the opportunity to make money in different market conditions, with a variety of underlying assets.

Another disadvantage of options trading is brought by the risks involved. Options trading can be particularly risky for beginner traders for their lack of experience. You need to understand each strategy required and to understand the risks that each carries before dipping your toes.

What Are Options Used For?

As you may have guessed from the sections above, options serve two primary functions: speculation and hedging.

Speculation is simply a gamble on the future price. In a case where a speculator predicts that the price of some stock will rise up, based on a technical or important investigation, the speculator will buy the stock or buy the call option on the specific stock. Speculation using a call option, rather than buying the stock outright, is useful to traders because the options contract gives them some leverage. For example, an out-of-money call option lets the speculator risk only a few cents or dollars, compared to if he would have purchased the stock itself at a high price.

The second reason, hedging, is the primary reason options were invented. Hedging is a sort of insurance policy that insures your other investments in stock or whatever asset, against a possible downturn. Hedging reduces risks down to a reasonable cost. For example, if you had bought stock and wished to bring down potential losses, you could do this using put options. The options would allow you to enjoy all the upside benefits while limiting the downside risks.

Chapter 2: Finding a Broker and a Platform

When it comes to finding the right broker and platform, the cheapest option is not always the best. You will find that spending some time evaluating brokers will guide you to the right choice, one that will give you quality services. With experience, you will also see that a diligent and reliable broker serves better, even if its fees are high compared to a cheap brokerage.

This chapter evaluates some of the factors you ought to consider when trying to find the right brokerage for your options investment needs.

What to Look for in a Broker

Discount Versus Full-Service Broker

Before going any further, you must first know that there are two kinds of brokers in the market: the self-directed discount brokerage and the full-service brokerage

The self-directed discount brokerage is the type that is built specifically to suit the needs of the self-directed or independent trader. In this case, the brokerage does not offer any investment advice but leaves the clients to make their own financial decisions. These brokerages only execute the clients' orders. For this reason, discount brokerages charge so much less than their full-service counterparts do.

The full-service brokers, the traditional brokers, are brokerages that provide a range of services at a fee. Among other services, these brokers give professional advice to their clients on the best investment opportunities.

Some brokerages offer a combination of full-service and self-directed services. Their services are ranked relative to the help that each investor category needs and the clients only have to choose, depending on the quality of services they need.

Most investors opt for the discount brokerages, and I presume that it is because anyone that gets into options trading must already have been running different investment instruments in the past and are knowledgeable in finance and investment matters, enough not to need a broker's help. They do this particularly when the broker's fee is measured by the number of trades performed rather than on the soundness of the advice a broker provides.

Fees and Commissions

One of the edges of competition for brokers is the cost of their services. Brokerages come up with creative ways to make money out of the activities of the traders, and you need to carefully examine the charges imposed before you settle for any single brokerage. Look at the contract fee and the per-trade fee.

The per-contract fee is the fee charged for every option contract signed in each trade, while the per trade is the minimum fee charged per transaction regardless of the number of contracts involved in each trade.

The total commission costs for each transaction is calculated using the following formula:

- Total Commission = $X for each trade + $Y per contract
- Here's another formula brokerages have taken up:
- Total Commission = Whichever is higher ($X for each trade or $Y for each contract)

- **Volume Discount**

Some brokerages offer discounts by charging a lower fee for a trading frequency that goes beyond a particular threshold. Therefore, if you plan to make numerous trades within the month, it makes sense to scout for a brokerage firm that has this discount scheme.

- **Limit or Market Order**

Some brokerages have differentiated fees for different kinds of orders; ensure that you take note of the charges for limit orders. Traders rarely make market orders.

- **Broker-Assisted vs. Internet Trading**

If you choose to trade with the help or guidance of your broker, it may cost you as much, or several times more than the independent internet trades. Therefore, to save on your costs, only choose broker-assisted trading when you know you will have no access to the internet because then, an excellent opportunity could come up, and you would need to take it up.

- **Disguised Fees**

Some brokerages charge low fees, but they make up for the low rates with some hidden charges. Therefore, if you come across a brokerage that charges unusually low fees in comparison to its competition, ensure that you look around to see whether the brokerage has placed some disguised fees.

Some of the hidden fees you ought to look out for include:

- *Minimum Balance Fee:* This is a periodical fee levied (every month or after every quarter) if your account goes below a set threshold.
- *Account Inactivity Fee:* Is the fee that some brokerages charge if the trader has not made any trade in a particular period of time.
- *Annual Maintenance Fee:* Is the fee that brokerages charge every year you hold an account with them, whether you have been making trades or not.

It is crucial that you give careful consideration to the commissions and fees charged because they have a significant impact on the profits or the losses you make, especially if your trading capital places a cap on the number of contracts you can make for each trade. For example, some brokers limit you to only having 1 or 2 contracts for each trade while others set the win/loss ratio to 6:4, or less. You need to know that a low-commissions broker is important because it can boost your earnings by up to 50%.

Quality of Service

While making consideration of the fees and commissions charged affects the profitability of your trading, this ought not to be the only consideration. Other factors such as the ease of use, execution speed, and site availability matter, particularly in the case of self-directed online trading, also determine the quality of services a broker provides.

Here's a brief description of why you should consider each of the factors mentioned above.

- **Ease of Use**

By themselves, options are already a complicated lot, and using a complicated platform or brokerage would only make things worse. However, an easy-to-use interface helps to make your activities smoother and to minimize errors. If the interface is not right, trading mistakes that would follow will cause the loss of large sums of money because money in the options market changes hands every day. Therefore, when looking for a trading platform, opt for one that offers all its resources on a single screen for easy access.

- **Quality of Execution**

The SEC, through the National Best Bid or Offer (NBBO), requires brokers to offer the customers the finest obtainable asking price in the market when they buy securities and the finest possible proposal price to traders seeking to sell securities. Ensure that your broker guarantees trade execution prices that meet or even exceed the SEC requirements.

- **Availability and Speed of Execution**

Perhaps the most important factors to consider when selecting a brokerage are the availability of the site and its responsiveness. Options trading is time-sensitive, and you need to execute your trades immediately an opportunity comes up. However low the commission, and the fees are, if you cannot make the trades, or the site takes too long to load and execute commands, taking up this site will only cause you to waste your resources. The amount you save in commissions and fees will not be worth it.

A responsive site ensures that your price quotes are timely. In this information age, information moves fast, across the globe, day, and night. As such, traders should be able to react to breaking news very fast. You will not want to be the trader that lags behind and only hears of opportunities when other traders have taken them up.

Kindly note that the speed of your internet determines the speed of execution. Therefore, ensure that you take up a package that guarantees speed. A broadband connection is faster than dialup. Before you get on to the brokerage site, ensure that your connectivity is good.

Free Education

If you are a newbie or a seasoned trader that wants to expand his knowledge of options trading strategies, education should be at the forefront of your considerations for possible brokerages. You must get a broker that offers educational resources in the form of live or recorded webinars, online options trading courses, face-to-face meetings with a mentor, and one-on-one guidance via phone or through online means.

You see, options trading is complex, and you may want to spend the first few months, or even years, on the student-teacher learning mode. Get as much education and training as you can. If you come across a broker who offers a simulated, virtual, trial version of the options trading platform, take up the opportunity and test-drive with the dummy account before you can place any real money on the line.

Quality of Customer Service

Customer service matters greatly. You wouldn't want to be stuck with a broker that does not respond to you, or if you make a request or inquiry, the broker responds days or weeks later. Reliable customer service is a priority item, especially for those that are new to options trading. Experienced traders conducting complex trades also need all the help they can get.

As you choose between brokers, think of the means of communication you would wish to have with the broker. Would you like to speak with them on the phone, via email or to meet them in person for a live chat? Is the trading desk on call during the stipulated hours? If you are not sure of this, make several test calls to potential brokers to gauge their availability and responsiveness. Are they available 24 hours 7 days a week, or are they only available during the week? Are the representatives with whom you speak knowledgeably about options and options trading?

Before you settle for any trading platform or broker, ensure that you reach out and ask a few critical questions. See the quality of answers you get, and the time it takes to get them. If the answers are satisfactory, having considered other factors discussed above, make your choice of brokerage.

Recommended Options Brokerages and Platforms

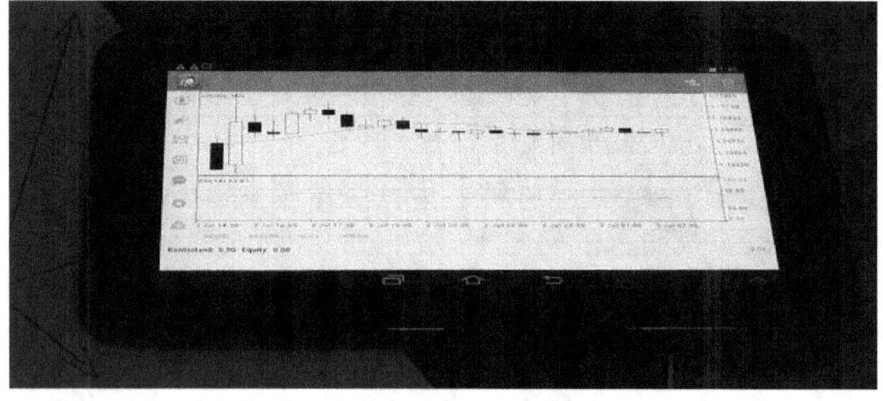

Below is a list of brokerages and platforms that offer the best options trading services. Read through this list to see the platform that is best suited for your options trading needs.

TD Ameritrade

TD Ameritrade is at the helm of the ranks thanks to its combination of desirable factors like having excellent education resources, and easy to use platform suited for traders of all levels, and reasonably priced services.

For each trade, TD Ameritrade requires its users to pay $6.95 and $0.75 for each contract involved in the trade. Traders also get to enjoy 60 days commission-free ETF, equity, and options trades to traders who place a deposit of $3,000 or more. The commission-free offer is available periodically, and you need to check whether it is currently available. Besides these benefits, TD Ameritrade offers a few more bonuses for clients with larger opening deposits.

Interactive Brokers

The Interactive Brokers platform has long been famed for its low-cost services. For a long time, this platform was thought to have a complex interface, and its customer service somewhat unreliable. Only hyperactive traders could use this platform.

Today, the situation has changed, and Interactive Brokers now extends its services to the less sophisticated and the less active traders. The company's trading platform, called the Trader Workstation platform, is now friendlier, easier to customize, and available either as a website or an app. The mobile app, in particular, does not need much typing because users can use voice commands and wheels to navigate the screen.

Interactive Brokers has also introduced a new feature called the iBOT to its platform. This application allows you to ask questions in English and get a direct answer rather than having to go through different features on the platform to get a response. For example, if you wanted to view the strike price and the expiry date of a particular option, you only have to say, "Show options chain for Company-X for the next two expirations."

Using the iBOT platform, traders can also set up a spread very quickly, and then extrapolate it into the future. The IB Probability Lab allows them to simulate possible trades before they can lay down real money.

Unfortunately, the IB platform only allows the streaming of its platform in one device at a time. This means that if you are using your mobile app to stream quotes, and you open the same on your computer, one of the platforms will automatically close, and you can no longer view the snapshot quotes. When it comes to fees and commissions, account holders with less than $100,000 deposit have to pay a minimum of $10 each month and may also have to pay additional fees to view real-time data. Traders also pay a fee of $0.0005 per share. Another downside of the platform is that its app form lacks some features.

Despite the disadvantages, Interactive Brokers remains one of the best options trading platforms because of its meager margin rates, numerous educational resources, and the fact that anyone can use it to trade. There is no set minimum account balance or the annoying per-leg base fee.

Robinhood

The Robinson trading platform is highly ranked because amazingly, it does not charge any commission. To a trader seeking to reap profits, it doesn't get better than free. Robinhood is an excellent app for beginner traders because it limits the risks to which they are exposed. This is because if you do not have to pay any trading fees, you only risk the money you set aside for your initial investment, and nothing more.

Although Robinhood does not offer much when it comes to research and educational material, if you had a rich educational resource, such as this book, you could refer to the knowledge in your book then practice your trading on the platform itself. This would be ideal for people who are starting options trading as a hobby.

For traders who have taken up other investment vehicles like ETFs, stock trades, cryptocurrencies, and ADRs (American Depository Receipts), Robinhood offers commission-free trades.

Lastly, since Robinhood is a web-first platform, traders get real-time notifications about the condition of the market, and this knowledge, they use to make trades and investments in their platform.

Lightspeed

This is a broker whose setup, the Livevol X, is designed to meet the needs of experienced very active options traders. The platform also offers a number of analytical tools like Skews Data and historical options Greeks, that other platforms do not provide. It also provides an array of analytical tools that scan the market to get a hold of different trading opportunities. In addition, its charting features are advanced and easy to customize to your needs and liking.

Once you get onto this platform, you can analyze your portfolio by grouping your positions under particular icons and symbols to determine the strategies that are currently active.

The Lightspeed platform also comes with a profit-and-loss risk graph to help you gauge the success of the strategies you have taken up. During trading surges, this broker was reported to perform very well, and to make trading very easy.

Since Lightspeed is a somewhat complicated platform, options trading newbies are advised to keep off it. Those who use it should also note that Lightspeed does not allow direct market access or futures trading in its platforms, both the web-based and the mobile app.

Overall, Lightspeed is an excellent app because of its terrific speed order execution software that also generates graphs to indicate price movement. The per-contract commissions are also very low, and there are no monthly or per-leg base charges.

Charles Schwab

The Charles Schwab brokerage runs a platform called the StreetSmart Edge. This platform can be accessed either by downloading it on your desktop or by simply accessing it in your browser. The StreetSmart Edge has numerous tools and content that help the user to build a spread by choosing the type of trade they need to place from its down-drop menu. Users can also choose the legs from the options chain exhibition feature on the platform.

The Idea Hub allows users to look for possible contracts going by their potential profitability and market activity, then arranges them into four options-specific categories. The categories include covered calls, big movers, premium harvesting, and earnings. Once you see the idea presented on display, click on it, and if favorable, click on Trade to fill your order ticket. If your option is low priced, you get to close it for free on this platform.

The Charles Schwab brokerage and its platform are best suited for the emerging options trader. You will only need to go through lots of education and support from the Schwab experts. You also will enjoy the low fees too.

Overall, Charles Schwab stands out because of its Idea Hub feature that gives you clues regarding actionable trading options in the market. It also offers trading lessons that advance as you grow in your trading. In addition, the options available are based on a wide array of asset classes.

The Charles Schwab brokerage and platform is one of the best trading platforms for beginner traders.

Chapter 3: Transaction Fees and Slippage

Transaction Costs

Transaction costs, also called transaction fees, are the charges related to the execution of a trade or the expression of an intention to maintain a position. As such, in options, the exchange gees, brokerage commissions and the Securities and Exchange Commission (SEC) fees count as the transaction costs.

Typically, brokerage commission is paid on a per-contract basis, and it pays for the services the trading platform renders like customer service and the execution of orders. The SEC fees are destined to take care of regulatory functions by the governing body. The exchange fees are a special fee to compensate markets for running a reliable and robust marketplace. If the investor wants to use his margin interest to complete a transaction, he must pay some margin interest. This makes margin interest the money that is charged for borrowing money from the brokerage.

Before you go ahead placing your order, ensure that you understand, and account for all the transaction costs that have to do with attaining and maintaining the position you have taken. The transaction cots affect much more besides the premiums you have paid or have received after the purchase or the sale of an option. Therefore, if you want to break even every time, ensure that you consider all variables involved in the trade, including the premium you paid at first, the option contract's strike price, and the transaction costs the brokerage firm charges.

Slippage

Slippage is the difference between a trade's expected price and the actual price at which the trade is executed. Slippage happens at any time in the year, but it is most prevalent in times of high volatility because that is when market orders are used. It is at that time that markets are highly volatile and susceptible to unexpected quick turns in a particular trend.

Slippage can also happen after a large order has been executed, although there is usually not enough volume at the time, and at that price, to maintain the current ask and bid spreads.

The change in price during a slippage is either negative or positive because it all depends on the direction the price has taken. It matters whether you are going short or long and whether you are closing or opening a position. As such, a slippage is any deviation from your trade strategy. Whichever direction the deviation heads, the slippage lowers the trader's confidence in the strategy's intended outcome.

If slippage is not well modeled, even a theoretically sound strategy could yield negative returns. If a seemingly positive winning strategy produces negative results, it means that the trader is yet to attain the best execution, and he may need to perform some auditing to determine the best execution policy. As such, proactively managing the slippage is likely to produce greater confidence in the overall trading strategy.

An example of slippage would be if you were closing a long position with the intended sale order placed at $100.20. If the order is executed at $100.15, you get a negative $0.05 slip. If the same order is completed at $100.25, it will have gotten a $0.05 positive slip.

If the slippage affects your positions, you still might be lucky to find some brokers who would be willing to fill your orders, but they can only do so at the worse price. However, the best trading platforms' execution practices ensure that once the price has shifted outside of your tolerance level, any time between when you placed your order and the time of execution, the order will be rejected. Their reason for doing this is to protect you from the adverse effects of slippage as you open and close your position. However, if the situation changes and the price moves to a better position, your brokerage would fill your order at the better, more favorable price.

Other ways to protect yourself from the effects of slippage is to install limits or some stop losses on your active positions. The limits help to avoid slippage as you enter or close your position because a limit order only fills at the price you have stipulated prior. On the other hand, the stop loss closes out your trade immediately; your asset's price hits the particular level you had specified. If the asset price is triggered, you are required to pay a premium.

When Does A Slippage Occur?

We have established that slippage occurs when there is high market volatility or low market liquidity. In a low liquidity market, the market participants are often very few, and this means that there are not many traders on the other end of a trade. In this case, it takes much longer to execute a trade because the seller often has to wait for a long time to get a buyer. In the course of the delay, asset prices change, and in a volatile market, this could happen in a split second; sometimes, in the few seconds, a trader will take to fill his order.

Slippages are most prevalent around the time when major news events are happening, such as when a major bank is announcing changes regarding its monetary policies or its interest rates. A major company announcing significant changes, such as when it presents its earnings reports or announces changes in its leadership, often produces the same result. Events like these increase market volatility and increase the possibility of experiencing a slippage.

Unfortunately, many of these significant events, like a company announcing a change in its leadership, are not often predictable. However, others like the reading of company financial reports, announcements by the central bank on different monetary policies, and major meetings like those of the Federal Reserve are scheduled, and traders can speculate what is to be talked about in those meetings. These predictions are not always right.

How to Avoid Slippage

Whenever it comes to managing slippage, consider taking only the best practices to limit the slippage risk. For example, now that liquidity leads to slippage, the best strategy is to counteract that liquidity. Come up with a strategy that accounts for the changing positions during the troughs and the spikes of the volatility. The strategy might involve limiting the number of market orders you place during periods of high-volume trading and increasing the number and sizes of the orders when the liquidity is low. This strategy will effectively reduce slips.

Another way to reduce slippage is to take up a more procedural and quantitative option that allows you to model for slippage. As you do this, you will iteratively improve the cost model with backtesting, which eventually limits your exposure to slippage.

Backtesting is a strategy that involves applying a particular trading strategy to historical data to see whether the strategy will produce accurate results. Backtesting is done to gauge the accuracy of any particular strategy. Many people use backtesting to gauge the profitability of the strategy using trading ratios like the risk-reward ratio and the win rate. They also rely on backtesting to unveil the underlying transaction costs in each strategy. As such, backtesting can effectively discern slippage because it is considered as part of the costs of doing business, just as it is used to discern other fees and commissions.

Backtesting is particularly common taken up when evaluating trading strategies used in the fields of production and development. Once a new strategy is developed, historical trade data is used to test the new strategy's slippage tolerance and the projected impact that slippage can have on the company's profitability. What's more, backtesting a currently running production or trading strategy, with the help of some adequate dataset, will also help to expose the strategy used to uncover some unrealized profits and to troubleshoot any underperformance. In either of these cases, the goal is to model the source of the slippage and to measure its impact, more accurately.

Overall, pinpointing the reasons and the trends that cause repeated slippage and inputting measures to minimize the errors and trends will minimize the slippage.

Other Strategies to Help Avoid Slippage

There are three other smart ways to minimize slippage and its effects on your trading.

Set up Some Limit Orders and Guaranteed Stops to Your Order Positions

Guaranteed stops, unlike other kinds of stops, are not subject to slippage, and will, therefore, ensure that your trade closes at the exact point you have set. This makes the guaranteed stops the ultimate way to manage risks when a market is moving against you. Keep in mind, however, that a guaranteed stop, unlike other stops, will require that you pay a premium once it is triggered.

Limit orders are also useful for mitigating risks that come with slippage as you enter a trade, and when you want to make a profit from a winning trade. When you have a limit order, your order will only be occupied at your predetermined price, even if the limit order is triggered.

Limit Your Trading Activity to Markets with High Liquidity and Low Volatility

If you keep to markets with low volatility and high liquidity, you will have avoided the primary causes of slippage: high volatility and low liquidity. Low volatility means that the price will not be changing too quickly, while a high liquidity market is one where there are many active participants on either side of the trades.

In the same way, you can also reduce the possibility of slippage if you limit your trading to the hours when there is the highest market activity because that is when the market is liquid. At this time, your orders stand a higher chance of being executed at your requested price, unlike when the market is less liquid.

The time when the US market is most liquid is when exchanges like the New York Stock Exchange and the NASDAQ are open. At this time, the trading volume is very high. The same is the case for the forex market because even though the market runs 24 hours every day, the best time to trade is when the London Stock Exchange is open.

If you ignore this rule and decide to hold positions when the markets are closed, such as during the weekend or at night, you are likely to suffer slippage. Slippage happens when the market reopens, and the prices have changed. The news, events of the night or morning, and other announcements will have had an effect on the financial market.

See How Your Broker Treats Slippage

If, when opening or closing a position, the price moves against you, some brokers might still execute your orders. However, this is not the proper thing to do because your broker should never fill your orders at a worse level than the one you have requested because it might be rejected.

A good broker sets a tolerance level on either side of your predetermined closing price, and if the market remains within this range at the time when the broker receives your order, your trade will be executed as the level you have requested. However, if the price steps out of this range, the brokerage does one of two things.

If the market shifts and the price is better, the broker will ensure your order closes at that better price so you can enjoy some additional profit. If, on the other hand, the market moves against you, beyond the brokerage's tolerance, the brokers ought to reject that order then ask you to resubmit your order it at the current level.

Chapter 4: Developing A Trading Strategy

The primary reason anyone invests is to 'make money,' but any seasoned options trader will tell you that there are other considerations to make. However, when it comes to options, there are other reasons, besides the desire to make a buck, for investing.

Investors use options to hedge against risks. Hedging is sort of like protecting or reducing the risks that the position you have taken attracts. While you may want to minimize losses, some of the strategies will also limit your profits, but others will not.

Traders also invest in options to manage risks. Managing is not the same as hedging. You see, hedging is protecting your investments from risks that could arise while managing is working to minimize the risks that already exist. This is the main reason traders turn to options trading.

Yes, you will get into financial trading with the intention of reaping profits, but options ensure that the risk of losing your investment capital is lessened. The strategy you choose will allow you to set a maximum loss limit for any trade, something that other investment vehicles might not allow you to do.

A stop-loss, for example, might be installed to control losses, but the losses can still fall further down, beyond the stop-loss price. The likelihood of earning more profits and the benefit of having your losses capped is what many traders appreciate about various options trading strategies.

Another reason for investing in options is to protect your investments against stock market surprises. Although the surprises do not happen very often, when they do, some are quite volatile and can be disastrous to the earnings of various stock market investors.

Lastly, investing in options is also meant to tweak the predictions made in regards to the stock market. This is particularly critical for experienced traders. For example, if a trader wants to adopt a bullish position relative to a particular index or stock, investing in options will allow you to reach your expectations.

Take Caution When Picking Using Trading Strategies

Before we get to the subject matter, it is important that I offer a word of caution to option traders, particularly the rookie traders. You should never place your hard-earned money at risk unless you are certain that you understand all the risks involved, and that you can see all the curves and corners of the strategy you want to take up.

Don't just take up the advice of those around you; do your part and study to see if the trade is suitable and that you can handle the risks that come with it. Understand all that it takes to make money using your chosen strategy, also know all the ways through which you can lose money, and when you are satisfied with your assessment, make the trade.

As you take up any options strategy, ensure that you firmly understand how that strategy works and have a clear understanding of the outcome or results, you hope to derive from managing the trade efficiently.

When dealing with options, put away the buy-and-hold mentality. Options should be traded, though not actively, but the expiry date should determine and hasten your exit. As an effective trade manager, or with the help of your broker, you ought to discern when a particular trade or a strategy is not working, and when you ought to walk out of that position. If you must suffer a loss, so be it. It would be negligent of you to hold a losing trade, one that would cost you your entire investment, in the anticipation that the trade will turn around and allow you to break even.

Developing a Trading Strategy

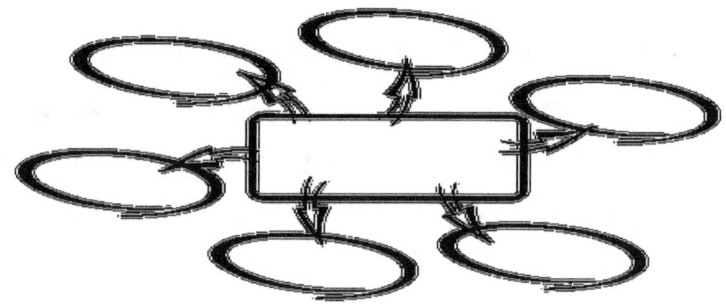

Most traders prefer using the already existing trading strategies because they are already proven, and you can already tell what the outcome will be if you apply the trading strategy appropriately. However, others like to take a different direction of creating their own trading strategies before they enter a position or on the go.

The good news is that coming up with a strategy is easy, but the challenge is to ensure that it is profitable. You will not, however, enter a new market and start making rules; you need to have studied and understood what works and what doesn't. Go over all the existing strategies, understand the indicators too, then use the knowledge you gather to charter your own path.

While starting out with high expectations is encouraged, thinking that the first trading strategy you come up with will bring supernormal profits and make you rich is unrealistic. Rarely do people get it right the first time, even with proven strategies. In addition, you will realize that profitable trading goes beyond the strategy you take up.

To develop your trading strategy, follow the following steps:

Build Your Trading Ideology

Before you put the clay in your hands, you must first have a good idea about what you are trying to make. Before you develop a strategy, you must first understand how the market itself works. The most critical of the questions you can ask yourself at this stage is, "What makes me think that I can make money from trading in the markets?" Think about why the financial market, and the options market, in particular, would be your suitable niche for your activities in comparison to other money-making activities.

The one secret to building wealth, one that I have come to treasure, is not to have a get-rich-quick mentality or to make plans in that regard. Do not believe any theories or claims that people make perfectly rational decisions.

Once you have worked on your ideology, everything else will be easier. You will make better decisions. Give them their due attention and ensure that you keep things as simple as possible. You do not want to come up with a strategy that will become too complex that it confuses you. Minimize the moving parts because the more they are, the harder it will be to manage or to make changes.

Identify Your Market

Of course, you want to trade options, which means that you will head for the options market. However, there are many kinds of options. Some are stock-based, others are index-based, and there are many more kinds. Which type do you want to trade-in? Go on and read about each and see the one that is best suited for you.

Assess Your Skills

How ready are you to trade? What do you know about trading? Do you have all the equipment needed? Have you figured out what you would do in each of the possible scenarios? Do you know how to use and read the indicators? Are you able to follow the signals? Are you confident that the knowledge you now have is enough to help you find your way through the market?

Trading is a give-and-take game. Do you know what is expected of you when you enter a particular position? Do you know what will be taken from you? Do you understand all the ways a situation could play out? Have you noted all the risks involved?

A wise trader will ensure that he has all these factors figured out and be prepared with the answers to each of these situations. Not having a plan will only amount to giving away your hard-earned money in the name of trading.

Choose a Suitable Trading Period

Before you head on to the market, you must decide on the most suitable time to do it. Are you available to trade? Will you have time to watch the market for an extended period? Will you be an active trader, or will you do trade occasionally? Choose to trade when you are available so that you pay keen attention to your trade. After doing this, some people actually realize that options trading is not for them.

Make Preparations in Your Mind

Is your mind prepared to take on the trading challenge? Are you ready? Are you physically, mentally, and emotionally ready for the battle in the market? If you are not ready, it is better to take some time off and resume trading later. If you don't, you risk losing your entire investment.

Mental preparation is essential because it ensures that you set away anger, resentment, the desire for revenge, preoccupation with other things, and other distractions are set aside so that you focus on the task at hand.

Once you start trading, the issues you face will not cease; you will still experience disappoints, losses, anger, and other distractions that would take your mind off the important issues of trading. When this happens, a mantra might help to get your mind in the right frame. Most seasoned financial traders have a market mantra they repeat before they begin their trading so that they can get their minds into what they're doing.

As you go into trading, come up with a mantra that will get you right in the trading zone. Also, ensure that your trading area does not have any distractions. Distractions could cost you greatly.

Set a Maximum Risk Level

As you get into trading options, how much of your capital will you be willing to risk at any given time? The amount of risk you can tolerate will depend on the trading style you have taken up and your risk tolerance. On any given trading day, ensure that your risk strictly stays within the 1% and 5% of your portfolio range. This means that if you lose that percentage amount in the morning, you get out and stay out the rest of the day. You do not go back to trading. It is better to retreat so that you live to fight another day.

Have Clear Goals

Your lack of goals would have you beaten and packing the day after you start options training. This is because, without goals, you will have no clarity regarding what you want, the minimum rewards or risks you are willing to take, or the profitability targets you want to reach.

Most traders set a target that they will not take a trade unless the potential profit they can reap from it is three times greater than the risk they will be taking up. Therefore, if you have placed your stop loss at 2 dollars per share, you ought not to make a profit of less than 6 dollars.

The per deal, weekly, monthly, quarterly, or annual profit goals you set will be a guiding light to help you assess how you are well or badly you are doing. Therefore, return to them regularly to see where you stand.

Conduct Some In-Depth Research

There is an unspoken rule that you ought to know everything that is happening in the field you specialize in. For example, when you take up options trading, you ought to know all that is happening in the options market, and by extension, the rest of the financial market. What is going on in the local financial market? What is the buzz in the overseas market? Is the market up or down? How is your underlying asset performing in the market? Gather all the relevant information available and use it to gauge the mood of the market, particularly before it opens.

If you come across some meaningful financial information, use it to determine the position you will hold in the market. If you find out that some important financial announcement or report is about to be released, think about whether it would be beneficial or not to trade ahead of the important report. Most traders prefer to wait for the report or announcement out and to see the effect it will have on the market before they take up any unnecessary risk.

Being a pro-trader does not mean that you should gamble. Lean towards probabilities and only take up the opportunities that are likely to bring you good returns.

Have Some Trade Exit Rules

Unfortunately, most traders focus their attention, up to 90%, on buy signals but do not give much thought to where, when, or how to exit a trade. When down, especially, the traders fear to exit because they do not want to take losses. However, if you cannot get over losses and move past a trade, you will likely not survive as a trader.

If your stop-loss is hit, it means that you were wrong in your prediction of the trend's likely direction. When this happens, do not take the loss personally. The reality on the ground is that the majority of the professional traders lose more trades than they win. However, by properly managing their portfolios and limiting their losses, they still end up making profits.

Before you enter a position, first take note of the trade that exists. Each trade should have at least two. The first is the stop loss to use in the event the trade turns against you. At what point will you put the stop? Put that information down instead of relying on some mental notes. Secondly, each trade ought to have a profit target such that once you get there, you will immediately sell a portion of your position, and your stop loss can be moved onto the rest of your position so that you breakeven whenever you wish.

What Are the Rules Governing Your Entry?

It is no coincidence that we talk about the exit before the entry because, as you will discover in the course of your trading, it matters more how a trader exits a position than how he enters it. Exits serve a much more important role than entries.

A sample entry rule is that if a particular indicator signals in regards to some options or other kind of asset, and you stand to make three times as much profit as the value of the stop loss, provided you are in support, you should go ahead and buy some contracts or shares.

Chapter 5: The Techniques to Control the Risk

Soon after getting into trading, most traders painfully learn that it only takes one or two mistakes or a few unexpected events for an entire portfolio to be destroyed. The key to avoiding that is to learn and to install measures that can control the risks to which you are exposed. It is also paramount that you understand how to manage your money properly so that you do not engage in trading habits that could bring you down.

Here are a number of techniques and practices to help you manage risk effectively:

Ease into Trading

On landing an opportunity that is so revitalizing, one that could usher you towards new levels of profitability while still protecting your current investments, 'ease into trade' is not the advice you would want to hear. However, although it sort of puts you down, it is one of the best pieces of advice because it reminds you to take caution as you take up the opportunity. You need to start slowly, then build your skills as you continue to interact with different factors in the field.

The learning period ensures that you do not risk so much that you would be thrown out of the trade. Also, since you will not be risking too much, you have the opportunity to test various strategies (all of them will be new to you anyway), so you can figure out the process of investment rather than only weighing the strategies by their potential results.

You must remember that in options trading, just like in any other craft, it takes time to make considerable profits. The beginning might be quite shaky, with a few mistakes here and there, but if you stay focused and work on perfecting your trade analytical skills and execution, the basics of options trading will become second nature to you. You will easily navigate the market, securing the winning trades, increasing your returns, and building your portfolio.

Although sticking to the basics at first could seem boring, keep in mind that every great champion or person that has achieved anything meaningful in life became successful because he or she first dwelt on the basics and made that knowledge the foundation of everything else that they know. Options trading is no exception.

To that end, I recommend that you start your trading with a virtual account. Most brokers have them. The simulation allows you to use the strategies and techniques you would use when operating a real account. You will be happy when you make successful trades and will beat yourself up when you make losing deals. Luckily, the money used in a dummy account is not real, which is good because you will get to learn and make mistakes without drilling a hole through your pockets. It allows you to go through the emotions and thrills that come with making live trades, and with that, you will be simulated into the training environment.

Get to see how well options trading might work for you. Some people get into it and realize that they need more training before they can venture into the real market, while others realize that options trading is not for them at all. Therefore, get started with a dummy account to see just how well you would work and survive in the options trading market before you enter with both feet.

Once you have been successful in conducting simulated trades, you will have built the confidence you need to make real trades. With only a few successful trades, the outlook of your portfolio will be changing. Your assets will grow.

Plan Your Trades

The famous Chinese military general, Sun Tzu, said that every battle is won even before it is fought. By this, he meant that it is the preparation, the planning, and the strategies took up that determine the winning team, but not the fighting. You might have also heard successful investors saying that you ought to plan the trade, then sell the plan. It would seem that in life, planning ahead makes the difference between failure and success.

Top among your priorities should be to investigate whether your chosen broker is down for frequent trading. Some brokers only attend to the needs of traders who do not trade frequently. If you do not intend to trade frequently, the broker would be good for you, but if you plan to be thoroughly engaged, getting with this broker would be a total mismatch. You see, the majority of the brokers who deal with irregular clients charge very high commissions, and for a regular trader, this would turn out to be too expensive. In addition, this type of broker does not offer any analytical tools.

Another angle to planning is to mark the stop-loss and the take-profit points of a trade. A trader should have determined how far he is willing to go in regards to the price, whether buying or selling. The reason is that they approach a trade having determined the possible returns from a trade, having weighed it out against the tendencies of the market. If the trader perceives that the returns will be high, he or she goes ahead and executes the trade.

In contrast, traders who do not take time to prepare and conduct research often end up unsuccessful. They get into trades without first identifying the points at which they will sell at a profit or a loss. Like a gambler who is on a lucky or unlucky streak, the trader's emotions begin to rise and take over, and trading decisions are made in a whim.

If the trader is making wins, he will be provoked to keep making more trades, and down this path, he could lose all that he has won. If the trader is making losses, the desire to make up for the losses with more trades overtakes, and this could just be the downward spiral that pushes him out of options trading.

Setting the Stop-Loss and the Take-Profit Points

The take-profit point is the price point at which a trader will sell his stock and take the profit. This happens when the trader perceives that given the risks, the chances of making more profits from the position he is holding are bleak. For example, when the stock price is approaching a resistance level, one that it cannot breakthrough, the trader may see it wiser to sell his options contract before the contract expires.

The stop-loss point is the point at which an options trader is willing to sell his contract and take in all the loss that comes with the decision. He does this when he perceives that the trade will not pan out as he had hoped. The stop-loss point keeps him from maintaining this position in the hope that the trade will turn around because, in most cases, this attitude often leads to many more losses. Therefore, when the trader checks out of the trade, he also avoids all the future losses he would have endured had he maintained his position.

As you may have guessed, the trader does not set the take-profit and stop-loss points out of guesswork; he has to have conducted in-depth technical analysis. The analysis also helps the trader get it right on the issue of timing to ensure that he does not lock out any possible benefits.

The moving averages are some of the most useful tools to help you determine your stop-loss and take-profit points. They are easy to calculate, too, in addition to being widely followed in the investment market. The key moving average is 5-, 9-, 20-, 50-, 100-, and 200-. If you set them against a stock's chart, you will be able to see how the stock price has reacted to them, whether they have been treated as support or resistance levels.

The take-profit and stop-loss points also fit well on the resistance and support trend lines. You can draw these trend lines by drawing a line that connects the previous highs or the previous lows, especially those that are above or below the average. Just as when you use the moving average, the key is to determine the level at which the stock price reacts to the trend lines when on high volume.

Using Options Spreads

An options spread is the combination of two or more positions on options contracts, using the same underlying security, to come up with one major trading position. Suppose you purchased money calls on particular stock but went ahead to also buy cheaper out-of-the-money calls on the same underlying stock, you will have created a spread, commonly called a bull spread.

When you buy both calls and create a spread, it means that you stand to gain if the value of the underlying stock were to go up, but that you would lose the money with which you bought the calls, some, or all of it, if the stock price failed to go up. The advantage of doing it, however, is that since you have written calls on the same stock, you get to control some, if not all, of the initial costs, and therefore, you can reduce the amount of money you spend trading.

All options trading strategies we discussed earlier make the use of spreads, and these spreads make for a very effective way of managing risk. For this reason, the strategies tend to be useful for reducing the costs that it takes to enter a position and for reducing the amount that a trader stands to lose. Unfortunately, while the trader gets to limit the risk to which he is exposed, he ends up limiting the profits they could make also.

All the benefits of the spreads we have covered above have to do with entering a long position. However, the spread is also good for reducing the risks involved when entering a short position. For example, writing your put options while it is in-the-money, you would receive a premium for these options. However, this would expose you to possible losses you would suffer in the event the stock's value declined. On the other hand, if you purchased out-of-money put options because they were cheap, you would have to make payment upfront. However, with your options contract, you would have prevented any further revenue losses that come with the fall of the stock price. A spread like this is called a bull put spread.

In both the in-the-money and the out-of-money scenarios described above, you can enter positions that will allow you to earn an income in the event the price moves away from you.

However, you will have managed to put a cap to the losses you would suffer were the price to move against you. This is the reason options traders constantly rely on spreads to manage risk.

Using Options Orders

One of the simpler ways of managing risks is to make your investments in the different kinds of orders that are available to you. In addition to the four major options contracts we discussed in the first chapter, there are a few others that you could invest in to help reduce your risk and reliance associated with one particular order type.

One example of the additional orders is a market order, which is filled at the best possible price during the time it is executed. This is the typical way to trade options, but in a volatile market, there is no way to determine the best possible price. Your order may get filled at a lower or even higher price than you anticipated due to high volatility. However, market limit orders, you can choose the maximum and the minimum prices at which you want your orders filled. By doing this, you are able to keep yourself from buying or selling your orders at prices that are less favorable.

Some orders allow you to automate your exit from a position so that it locks in the profit you have secured, or it cuts off further losses from a trade that is not going well. You are only required to install a stop order, trailing stop order or a market stop order so that you retain control of the point at which you would wish to exit a position.

Diversification ensures that you are eating from all angles where profits are available. It helps you avoid missing potentially profitable positions and keeps you from holding on to positions that bring losses for too long, in the hope that the situation will turn around so that you close out of a bad position early enough. With options orders, you are able to limit the risks to which you are exposed to every trade you make.

Position Sizing to Manage Your Money

Before you manage the risks that come with investing, you must first properly manage the money you are investing in. There is not one without the other. Any investor has a limited amount of money to invest. Hence, it is important that he keeps a short leash in regards to where he is placing his money. Therefore, ensure that you do not lose sight of your budget so that you will not find yourself out of the ring.

The best money management strategy when trading is position sizing. This is a fairly simple concept, and it involves deciding on the maximum amount of capital you would want to invest before you enter into any given position. If you have taken up diversification, you must also ensure that you carefully calculate the amount you wish to invest in each venture, and take note of it in percentage, relative to your overall investment capital.

Position sizing facilitates diversification because it ensures that you are only using a small percentage of your trading capital in any single trade. Doing this helps to reduce your reliance on a single investment outcome and offsets losses made. You can be certain that even with years of experience, you still will be making trading mistakes, one time or the other. To ensure that the losses and the bad breaks don't turn you into a sad discouraged emotional trader, diversify your options trading investments. Venture into other investments also like stocks, ETFs, futures, real estate, and any other you fancy.

Diversification also ensures that in times of bad trades, you are not completely wiped out because you can use the returns from one trade to offset the losses of another trade, you will still have some money to buy your contracts when the bad trade turns around and becomes profitable.

Chapter 6: Credit Spread Strategy

When it comes to trading options, a trader has many options spread strategies from which he can choose. As we defined in the previous chapter, a spread refers to the purchase and sale of two or more options that have the same underlying asset in an attempt to take advantage of opportunities at both ends of a trade.

Spreads are classified in different ways, but the most basic of them is one that tries to figure out whether the strategy is a credit or debit spread. A credit spread, also called a net credit spread, is a spread strategy that has to do with the net receipts of premiums while a debit spread is one that involves net premium payments.

The Credit Spread

When creating a credit spread, the trader sells or writes a high-premium option and at the same time, buys an option with a low premium. The premium that the trader receives from writing the option is often more significant than the premium he pays to get the low-cost option. The difference is credited to the seller's trading account. When traders use the credit spread strategy, the maximum amount they receive, the one that is credited to their account when the position is entered, is called the net premium.

Looking at an example, let's say a trader takes up the credit spread strategy and writes a November call option whose strike price is $25 for $2, then simultaneously buys another November call option whose strike price is $30 for $1. Taking the usual multiplier, 100 shares per stock, then the net premium received will be $100, got from ($200 - $100). The trader will also enjoy more profits if the spread narrows.

When a trader is bearish, he is hopeful that the stock prices will go down, and he opts for long call options with a particular strike price before proceeding to sell a short all option within the same class, at a lower strike price. A bullish trader is often optimistic that the price of the underlying stock will go up and opts to buy call options at a particular strike price before proceeding to sell an equal number of call options at a higher strike price. The call options must be of the same class and have the same expiration.

The Debit Spread

We must mention a few details about the debit spread for your knowledge. A debit spread involves purchasing an option whose premium is high and selling one whose premium is low, simultaneously. The premium the trader pays for the long option of the spread is more than that of the written option.

The outcome of a debit spread is a debited premium, unlike the outcome of a credit spread. It is paid from the investor's account immediately; the position is opened. Because of this, traders use debit spreads to offset the costs that come with owning long options positions.

Let's see an example. Let's say a trader has purchased a March put option whose strike price for $15 is $3 and immediately purchases another March put option whose strike price of $10 is $1. The trader will have paid $2, or rather, $200, for the trade. Were the trade out-of-the-money, using the debit spread would have made for an excellent choice because it would have reduced the trader's maximum loss to $200 from $300.

Credit Spread Characteristics

Credit spreads have several unique characteristics with which you can differentiate them from other options trading strategies. They include:

- *Credit Spreads Are Useful Risk Management Tools*

We noted, in a previous chapter, that traders use spreads as tools to manage risk. In particular, credit spreads enable the traders to limit the risks to which they are exposed substantially by making them forego a limited profit potential. With the spread, traders can calculate the total amount of money they are risking even before they enter a particular position.

- *Credit Spreads Enhance Trading Versatility*

Traders are able to identify a combination of contracts to take either a bearish or bullish position by doing one of two things. First, they have the option of establishing a credit put spread, which is a bullish position whose short put has more premium. Second, traders can choose to create the credit call spread, a spread that takes a bearish position and has more premium on its short call.

Now, let's have an in-depth look at each of the strategies mentioned above:

The Credit Put Spread

Instead of outright selling your uncovered put options, traders take up the credit put spread. You see, selling an uncovered put option is a bullish move that is best taken when you expect the price of the underlying index or stock to go up. Traders sell the uncovered put option to generate income and then wait for the time limit to expire so that the option can be termed worthless. Although the risks involved when traders do this are somewhat limited, they can be substantial. The trader continues to lose money right until the value of the stock falls to zero.

Just like other spreads, the credit spread involves purchasing and selling options contracts simultaneously. Usually, the options are of the same class (whichever puts or calls) and riding on the similar underlying security. However, for vertical credit put spreads, the strike prices are different, although the expiration month is similar.

Also note that whenever you take up a bullish position using the credit put spread, the premium you receive for the option sold is higher than the premium you pay for the option. The result is that trading the option generates an income, although the amount will be less than what you would have got had you taken the uncovered call position.

Let's see an example. Suppose you buy 20 Company X March 65 puts each at $1 then sells 20 Company X March 70 puts each at $3, you will have a net credit of $2. In this case, the spread will be executed at $ 4,000 (($3 premium received - $1 premium paid) * (20 contracts each carrying 100 shares)).

If the market price of Company X shares closes above $67, you will make a profit. However, you will only maximize your profit (at least to get to $4,000) if the shares close at $70 and above. You will end up losing money if Company X's shares price goes below $67. For example, if the price fell to $65 or below, you stand to lose up to $2,000.

Kindly remember that taxes, fees, and commissions, though not included in this example, will affect the outcome of the trade, and ought to be factored in.

A trader would opt to take up this trade with the March 70 puts uncovered. Well, this could have resulted in a higher profit, $2,000, rather than the $1,500 profit received using the credit spread put. However, it is worth risking the $500 because the spread limits the risks involved significantly.

Had you sold the March 70 puts uncovered, essentially, your loss potential could have been a staggering $67,000 ($70,000 spent on buying the stock - $3,000 received on selling the puts), but that would only be if the company X stock value fell all the way to zero.

The credit spread scenario now appears better because under no circumstance can your maximum loss exceed $2,000.

Credit Call Spread

Usually, traders use credit call spreads instead of outright selling uncovered call options. Selling uncovered call options is a bearish trading strategy that traders can use when they expect the value of the security or the index underlying to go down. The goal of taking the credit call spread strategy is to generate income that could have been raised had the trader directly sold the uncovered call option and waited for the option to expire or become worthless.

Whenever you use the credit call spread to open a bearish position, the premium you pay for it will be lower than the premium you will receive once the option is sold. For this reason, the income you will generate using the credit call spread will be less than the income you would have raised had you taken an uncovered position.

The workings of the credit call spread are just like those of the credit put spread except that the loss and profit regions are on opposite sides of the breakeven point.

The Iron Condor

This is another type of credit spread for trading options, and it is the combination of the two strategies discussed above. The short iron credit option, for example, is a combination of the put credit spread and the call credit spread. For this reason, the iron condor position is neutral in regards to direction, and that it is most effective if the price is bound between the two spreads with time.

Here's a summary of the characteristics of the iron condor. It is directionally neutral, and the profits are only realized if the price maintains its position between the two spreads. The iron condor strategy gets better, or profits, with as time decays. The maximum profit a trader can derive from the iron condor is the credit received multiplied by the 100 shares of each option contract. The maximum loss is calculated by finding the difference between the width of the wider spread and the credit received, then multiplying the result by 100 ((Wider Spread Width – Credit Received) * 100).

To find the breakeven price using this strategy, find the upper limit by calculating the sum of the short call strike price and the credit received (Short Call Strike Price + Credit Received). The lower limit, you will get by finding the sum of the short put strike price less the credit received (Short Put Strike Price – Credit Received).

Advantages of Credit Spreads

- The margin requirement a trader needs is significantly lower than the one linked to uncovered options
- Spreads are useful tools for lowering risk substantially in the event the stock dramatically shifts against you
- The spreads limit the possible losses so that you do not lose more money than the margin requirement you have in your account when you enter your position. This is not

the case with uncovered calls because, with them, you stand to lose even more than your initial marginal requirement.

- Spreads are adaptable because they have a wide range of expirations and strike prices, and most traders can find combinations of contracts that they can take up for their bullish or bearish positions, for both the credit and the debit spreads.

- Credit and debit spreads do not require as much monitoring as other trading strategies do. Once you have established your strategy, the spreads, you can continue holding your position until expiration. However, they still may require some occasional review to certify that holding them up to when they expire is still beneficial. For example, if the underlying stock's price changes as fast or as far enough, the trader may still have the opportunity to close his spread position at a net profit, so long as the expiration date is yet.

Disadvantages of Credit Spreads

- The amount you send on the long option section of the spread reduces your profit potential.

- Since a spread requires the trader to choose two options, the cost of establishing both is high, even more than the commissions paid on a single uncovered position.

Chapter 7: Covered Calls

What Is A Covered Call?

A covered call is a financial market transaction that involves selling call options and simultaneously owning the equivalent amount of its underlying security. For example, if an investor already possesses a long position on an asset, then he sells call options of the underlying asset, raising higher profits than if he had only invested in one of them. The long position becomes the cover because the seller can deliver the shares in the event the call option buyer chooses to exercise it. Simultaneously buying a stock, then writing call options against that same stock is called a 'buy-write' transaction.

The covered call is a neutral strategy, and the investor takes it up when he expects only a small change, increase, or decrease, of the price of the underlying stock price within the life of the written call option. This approach is also suited for when an investor has a short-term neutral assessment of the asset he is holding, because of this, he clutches his asset for long but takes a short position by taking the option so that he can generate some income once he sells or writes the call option. He will receive a premium.

To put it in a simpler way, if an investor means to embrace the underlying stock for a long time but doesn't think such a substantial inclination in the price of the asset he is holding, in the near future, at least. The trader will seek to generate income by selling the option to receive a premium as he waits out to see how the market behaves.

As such, the covered call acts as a short-term hedge in regards to the long stock option and allows the investor to earn some income through the premium he gets. However, this is a trade-off because the investor forfeits the gains he would have received from the stock had the price moved above the option's strike price. If a buyer selects to exercise the option, after all, the trader who wrote the option is obliged to provide 100 shares for each contract he sold.

If an investor is very bullish or very bearish about the market, a covered call is not useful. Instead, if the investor is feeling very bullish, he would be better off not marks this option and should just hold the stock option. The reason is that option will cap profit the investor could have received if the stock price goes up, and this will decrease the total profit of the trade.

In the same way, if the investor is very bearish, he is better off just selling his stock because the premium he will receive for writing a call cannot do much to offset the loss he would suffer were the stock to plummet.

The maximum profit a trader can derive out of a covered call is equal to the strike price of the short call option in addition to the premium received for writing the call. The smaller the purchase price of the underlying stock. The greater the cost a trader can suffer in the acquisition price of the underlying stock, the lesser the premium collected.

If an investor wants to exercise an options contract (can be done at any time when dealing with US options, but on expiration if trading European options), trader sells his stock at the strike price, then if a buyer doesn't exercise the option, the trader (seller) gets to retain his stock.

As we have mentioned, a covered call, when sold, will typically be out-of-the-money, which permits profit to be made, both on the options contract and on the sale of the stock, but only if the stock price is maintained beneath the strike price of the option. On the other hand, a trader is certain that the stock price will decline, and still wants to keep his place, for the meantime, the trader may sell an in-the-money call option. The trader will collect an elevated premium for his call option, but the price of the stock will decrease lower the in-the-money strike price. Or else, the buyer of the option is entitled to collect the shares in contract traded so long as the share price is overhead the strike price of the option during expiration.

The Making of a Covered Call Trade

The first thing you must take note of is that when you purchase a stock, you should ensure that you purchase it in loads or bundles of 100-shares. When you vend the call contracts, sell it in 100-shares lots. For example, if you own 600 shares, you ought to sell them in 6 call contracts as opposed to the position you hold. You can likewise choose to sell fewer than 6 so that in the event the buyer exercises the call option, and you will not lose all your stock. If you sell 3 contracts and the buyer exercises the option, you will only lose 300 shares and still have 300 more shares.

When you write a call, you should wait for it to expire or to be exercised. If a contract expires, you get to make money off the premium the buyer pays. If the buyer does not exercise the option, you stand to keep the entire premium, and you can purchase back the option. However, there really is no good purpose to repurchase it.

The advantage of a covered call is that selling it helps offset the downside risks and adds up to the upside return. The risk, however, is that call sellers have to hold on to the underlying assets, lest they are holding naked calls.

Naked calls theoretically have a limitless loss probability if the underlying security goes up. So, if a seller wants to sell the contracts or shares, he must buy back option positions before they expire. Doing this increases the cost of transactions and lowers the net gain or the net losses from the trade activities.

Overall, covered calls are used to help gain income and to decrease the cost basis from shares or futures contracts.

Example of a Covered Call

Let's say an investor is in ownership of Company K shares and after analysis, the investor is optimistic about the long-term prospects of the company and its share price, but the investor feels that in short term, a stock is possible to trade flat, but maybe only within a few currency of its present value, say $20.

If the investor sells a call option on Company K shares whose strike price is $22, the trader will earn a premium from this sale but will cap the upper side on the stock to $22. In this case, one of three scenarios is likely to happen.

First, the shares might trade at a strike price below the $22, and if this happens, the option will be exercised useless, and the trader gets to retain the premium he received from the option. In this, the covered call approach will have helped the trader positively outperform the stock, and the trader will continue to own his stock and have an extra amount, the premium less the fees and commissions charged.

Secondly, Company K shares could fall, and the option will become worthless after expiry. The investor gets to keep the premium he received when he sold the options contract, and this helps to offset the decline he suffers when the stock price falls.

The third possible scenario is that Company K shares could rise above the $22 strike price. If the option is expired, the advantage of the stock will have been sealed at $22, but if the price goes higher, the sum of the strike price and the premium, it would have been better if the investor had held on to the stock alone. However, if the investor had intended to sell his shares at $22, he will have earned an extra amount, the premium he received.

Calculating the Rewards and Risks of a Covered Call

Covered calls are not without risks. The risk particularly comes from bearing a stock position whose price might decrease. The greatest cost a trader can suffer, however, is that which will be when the stock gets to zero. The maximum loss is calculated as follows:

Maximum Loss per Share = Premium Received + Stock Entry Price

E.g., Purchased a stock at $10 per share and on selling your call option, you receive a $0.02 option premium per share. The maximum loss you could suffer from your investment is $9.98 per share. The money you will have received as a premium reduces the maximum loss you would have suffered from owning your stock. However, selling your call option also limits the upside of your investment.

When using a covered call, your profit from the stock is limited to the strike price of the options contracts that you sold. The maximum profit you can reap from your trading is calculated as follows:

Maximum Profit = (Stock Entry Price – Strike Price) + Option Premium Awarded

Let's see an example. Suppose you bought a stock at $10 per share, and you sold it at $10.50 strike price, in addition to receiving a $0.05 premium. So long as the stock price remains at $10.50 at the time the option expires, you will maintain your stock position. However, if the stock price gets to $12, you will only receive whatever you gained up to $10.50. Your profit will remain $ ($10.50 - $10.0).

In the event you sell a call option, for you to maintain your shares, the value of the underlying stocks must fall beneath the call's strike price. If this happens, you will face a loss on your stock position, although the shares remain yours. However, the premium you will receive will help to offset your loss.

Generally, covered calls are considered a low-risk trading strategy, but it demands specific market conditions to work effectively. The best market condition in which to take it up is when the market is moving sideways, or when the market is moving up, slowly.

When a market is moving up or down quickly, the covered call trader will have problems. If the stock is moving up too quickly, the call option that was sold will be in-the-money, and the trader who wrote the option will have to give up his shares or to buy back the call options at a loss, as we have pointed out in the examples above. If the trader gives up his shares, but the stock goes on to increase in value, the trader will want to buy back his shares, but he will do so at a higher price.

On the other hand, if the stock is moving downward too quickly, the credit taken from the option will not be enough to cover the loss in value that the stock will experience over time.

You must understand, however, that no trading strategy and before you take up any of them, you must first take note of all potential risks.

Chapter 8: Strategies for Selling Covered Calls

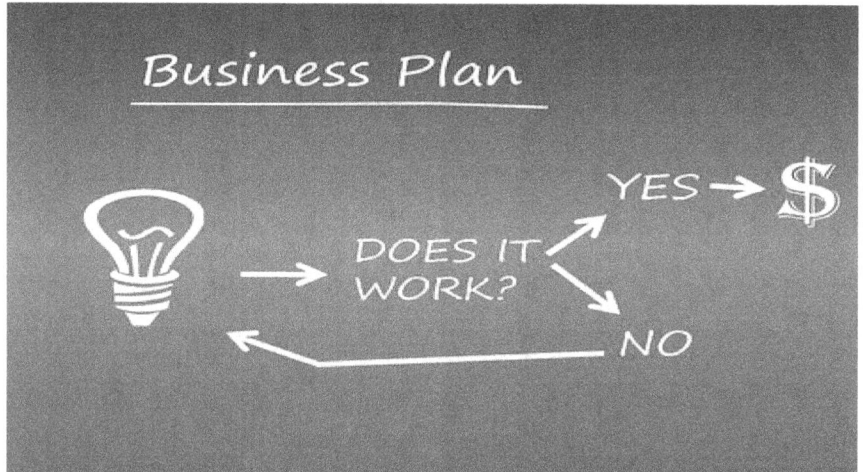

Strategy for Picking and Selling a Covered Call

When you sell or write a covered call, you give away your right to buy a stock you own, at a particular price, and within a stated time. From the sale, you pocket the premium, and this amount acts as a cover for when the stock value increases above your strike price.

As you choose a stock from your portfolio, settle on one that has already performed well, but one that you wouldn't mind giving up if the call option was assigned. Avoid picking stocks that you feel very bullish about in the long-term, and that way, you will not be too discouraged when you have to give up stock and end up not receiving any net returns from your investment.

Once you have settled on a stock, it is time to pick the strike price with which you are comfortable selling the stock. Typically, your strike price should not be out-of-the-money, because the goal is to see the price of your stock rise further before you give it up. You must pick an expiration date also, the date by which your call option will be termed worthless. 30 to 45 days from now would be an excellent starting point but trust your judgment more. Select a date that would allow you to have a decent premium if you sold the option at your chosen strike price.

Do not struggle when deciding on an acceptable premium. Some traders fear that they are either selling themselves short or being greedy. One rule of thumb among investors is that an acceptable premium is one that is approximately 2% of the value of your stock. You must remember that options are sensitive to time decay. Therefore, the further you go in time, the more valuable your call option will be. However, going so far in time will make it harder to predict the market trends, and the investors will be apprehensive about taking up your options.

As you will realize in your consecutive trades, the time value is a good indicator of the viability of an option. If you notice that a premium is abnormally high, there must be an underlying sensitive reason behind it. Go on into the market and find out. Search for information in the news also, and find out what could be affective the stock price. Most times, when something looks too promising, it is.

The Three Possible Outcomes of Writing Your Covered Call Options

Your sale of covered call options could produce three different outcomes:

The Stock Price Could Go Down

If after the sale, at the time the option expires, the stock has gone down, your call option will expire worthless. The good news is that you get to keep the entire premium you received when you sold it. The bad news, however, is that the value of your stocks will be down. When the stock price is down, the risk lies in the stocks, not the options part. However, the profit you got when you kept the premium will help offset the value loss.

If the stock price falls before the options expire, do not worry. The fall will not lock you into your position. Although you will have lost in terms of the value of your stock, the value of the call option you sold will have fallen too. This is not bad at all because you now have the opportunity to buy back your option for less than you were paid for it. If you no longer fancy the option on your stock, just close your stock by buying back the low-priced option you sold and get rid of the stock.

The Stock Price Could Go Above the Strike Price

If the stock price goes above the strike price on the day of expiration, the call option will be assigned to you, and you will have to give up 100 shares from your stock. If the value of the stock now rises again after you have given up your shares, too bad for you because you will miss the gains from the price rise. You will have already committed yourself, on the basis of your conscious decision to part with the stock at the strike price. When this happens, dust yourself and move on, promising that you will make a better decision next time.

The Stock Price Remains the Same

In this scenario, the price of the stock could remain as is, or rise just a tiny bit. This is not a bad situation because the call option you sold will expire, and you get to keep all the money you received as premium. The underlying stock might also give you a few dollars as returns. Be happy that you get to keep your returns and your stock.

Here's a summary of the strategy for picking and selling call options as described above:

- Pick a low volatile stock
- Buy call options when in-the-money
- Sell your call option when out-of-the-money

Assignment to Sellers of Call Options

If a purchaser selects to exercise the option, your shares of stock might be collected from you, as we mentioned above. We use the word 'might' because it is not guaranteed that you would be asked to deliver your shares; it all depends on whether you are assigned.

The assignment process works through a random lottery system that the Options Clearing Corporation (OCC) runs. When an exercise notice gets to the OCC, the OCC assigns it to a member clearing firm, the brokerage. The brokerage then assigns exercise notices randomly to various short options in their books. You may or may not be assigned. It is possible that you will escape the assignment. However, if the call option is in-the-money, with more than a few cents, the likelihood of escaping this assignment is very low. In all this, whether the option is out-of-the-money or in-the-money, the call buyer retains the right to exercise or not to exercise his option at any time before the expiration, whether it makes sense or not.

Tips for Selling Covered Options

Think About the Volatility

It is best to take up the covered call strategy when dealing with stocks that exhibit medium implied volatility. For this, you will want to choose a stock that can move, but in a sort of predictable direction. If the implied volatility is low, don't expect to get much in terms of the premium. If the implied volatility is high, you will have the pleasure of getting higher premiums.

Unfortunately, when the volatility of the stock is high, the stock price could go either way, significantly. If the prices increase, your chances of having your stock called away increases, but if the stock price drops sharply, you stand to make a significant loss. Once the price rises too high and the buyer exercises his option so that your stock is called, you cease to be a stockholder, assuming you had traded in options for that represent all your shares.

As you see, neither of the extremes is good; it is best to work with medium volatility because it will make getting the premium for the call you write worthwhile. It also brings down the unpredictability that comes with high volatility. Therefore, be wise in choosing the premium amount that will make the strategy you have taken worthwhile.

If assigned, Do Not Panic

If what you dreaded comes to be and you are called to give up your stock, it may be surprising and upsetting to have to give up a long-held stock position. Luckily, in that situation, you have more choices than you know.

Suppose you have continually invested in Company G's shares, 100 shares each year, over the past 10 years, and each year, the price was higher than the price in the previous year. It then happens that you write one covered call that goes against your holdings.

If you are assigned, you get to choose the lot of shares you want to give up from the lots you have been accumulating over the years. It would serve you better to give up the most expensive of them, the ones you bought the latest, and to keep the less expensive ones you purchased earlier. By doing this, you will have avoided triggering a large tax bill that is charged on the capital gains of your stock. However, when this time comes, ensure that you seek the help and advice of your tax professional.

If you hold your stock close and are not willing to let any of it go, that is still okay. Instead, head on to the open market, buy stock on the margin and deliver it instead. When you do this, you will have better control of your long-term stock positions and of the tax consequences that will come up. However, keep in mind that if you choose to deliver the newly purchased shares, you will need to have anticipated your assignment so that you buy the new shares before the assignment notice.

It is also true that purchasing on-the-margin stock carries its own risks. Essentially, the margin is a line of credit for purchasing stock for which a trader makes a down payment and pays the broker an interest rate. Trading by this margin is risky because if suddenly the market moves against you, you will be required to add more money to the down payment you made, in what is called a margin call.

Think of Buy-Writes

Some people use covered calls to make some consistent income. They buy the stock then sell the call option in a bid to make some money, all in one transaction. This strategy is called the buy-write.

A buy-write offers many benefits. For one, it is convenient because the trader does not have to head back to the market after making the transaction. The strategy also reduces the trader's market risk by preventing legging. Legging into a trade is getting into a multi-leg options trading position by getting into more than one transaction. Since a lot can happen as the trader moves from one trade to the next, even when they are just a few minutes apart, legging can happen, and it complicates the situation while adding onto the risks to which a trader is exposed.

As such, allowing yourself to get into a multi-leg position can be quite tricky. Most of the time, traders have to pay two commissions and go through tough tax treatment, which depends on each individual's situation. However, before you take up a buy-write, consult a tax advisor.

Come Up with a Plan for When the Situation Turns Against You

If you are bullish about a stock, in the long-term, you would typically write a covered call. However, this call too, can go south, and you will need a plan to control the damage. Unlike what people believe, in this situation too, you will have a number of choices from which to choose.

Unlike what many investors assume, selling your call does not limit you to one position up until the call expires; you could always buy back your call and take away your obligation to give up your stock. We have mentioned this already.

The situation is different if you realize that the price of the stock has fallen since you sold the call. You might have the opportunity to purchase your call back, although this will be at a price lower than the initial sale price. Doing this will allow you to make a profit on your position.

If you want, you can also dump your long stock position, and this will prevent further losses, particularly if the stock continues to drop.

Make a Comparison Between If-Called and Static Returns

Covered calls are a smart way to earn an income out of your long stock positions beside the dividends that the company's payout to shareholders. The if-called and static returns enable you to figure out whether selling your call would be a smart move for your investment plan.

Static returns refer to the scenario where your covered call and the stock do not budge, giving you the right to keep the premium paid as part of your income. The if-called return assumes that you will be assigned and that you will have to give up your stock.

Before you take up the covered call strategy, ensure that you consider both scenarios described above. The numbers therein are important because they will ensure that you continually work towards reaching your investment goals. When you do this, you will be happy with your investment returns and whichever way the situation turns out.

Mistakes Investors Make When Selling Covered Calls

Factors like unpredictable markets often lead investors to make mistakes in their quest to build a profitable portfolio. Here are some of the mistake's traders make:

Selling Their Options Naked Rather Than Covered

In the case of covered calls, the premium marks the maximum profit a trader could receive. If the value of the underlying asset significantly increases, and the investor does not own stock of the underlying asset, the investor could suffer high losses. A call option without an underlying stock is called a naked call, and it is very risky because its upside potential is limited while its downside potential is unlimited.

As such, investors must purchase shares on the underlying stock before the option expires. Depending on the underlying stock's market cost, buying the stock could dig a large hole in your capital and end up in losses. Therefore, if an investor wants to take up the covered call strategy, he should mainly focus on selling covered calls on stocks he or she already owns or can afford to purchase.

Selling at Expiration or at the Wrong Strike Price

One of the critical trading mistakes options traders make is to sell the calls on the day they expire, or at the wrong strike price, having not fully understood the rewards and the risks that come with each move.

The strike price greatly influences your profitability. Therefore, when you choose your strike price, first consider your desired payoff, and the amount of risk you are willing to tolerate.

The strike price of an out-of-the-money call will be higher than the present value of the stock, while the strike price of an in-the-money option is less than the market value of the stock. When you sell an in-the-money option, you get to collect more premiums, and you increase your chances of being called away.

The expiration date is also very important. Lately, options expire after a week, a month, a quarter, and a year. A longer dater option gets a greater premium because its time of decay is far off. However, call sellers benefit more from shorter-term options.

Failing to Have A Loss-Management Plan

Most traders are not prepared for the reality that the trade could very well move against even their best predictions. Although no one goes into a trade hoping that it will go wrong, you should be ready for this possibility, and take measures to manage the risks that come with that.

Primarily, a plan to manage losses involves having an outlay of the money you are willing to risk in your trade even before you enter a position. You also should know how you will bail out of a trade if it goes the other way, so you may have a definite plan to help you cut your losses.

As you make your plans, it also makes sense to have a realistic picture of the profit you will be targeting. This, you will gauge by looking at the historical movement of your underlying asset, and you should leave enough room to wiggle should the market become unstable, and the stock prices start to fall or rise drastically.

Be careful that there isn't one loss-cutting strategy that will suit all trading scenarios; each trading style will need a new damage control strategy. Besides your style of trading, the size of your account and the position size will also matter.

The advantage is that when trading options, you get great flexibility. For instance, you may opt to buy back your option to relinquish your obligation to deliver your stock.

Only remember that when you notice that a trade is moving against you, the best strategy is not to add more money to it, stick to what you were doing and accept the loss. Keeping your emotions in check is critical in financial trading.

Failing to Factor in the Dividends

Dividends are an important consideration when it comes to evaluating option prices in your quest to choose the right stock. If you buy 100 shares, you will receive dividend payments if the company makes them out, so long as the ex-date comes before the day the contract expires. This is besides the premium you will receive when you sell your call option.

Undoubtedly, dividend payments will affect the call premium. The dividend payment causes the stock price to fall, and as such, the call premiums fall too, although the put premiums become higher. Therefore, if you are expecting dividend payments, it is better to exercise your call option early.

Expecting Returns Immediately

Options are not necessarily a short-term investment strategy; traders can also use them for long-haul investments. However, when they do this, they should not expect immediate returns. Options can be quite profitable, but they are by no means a 'get-rich-quick' strategy. Realizing the returns you want takes time. Realistically, traders should aim for 10 to 12 percent annual returns.

In addition, traders should have a plan that caters to the possibility of receiving lower returns than what they had expected. However, for the most part, they ought to have a consistent strategy, one that will produce consistent returns for the coming years.

Chapter 9: Advanced Strategies for Buying Calls

This chapter on advanced strategies for buying call options assumes that the trader already has a basic understanding of the fundamentals of options trading. As such, the strategies discussed herein are advanced. However, when it comes to financial trading, it all goes down to buying and selling call or put options at a particular strike price, with an expiration date attached. Therefore, the strategies are all about setting up different building blocks to guide you as you buy call options.

The advanced strategies are divided into four categories: bullish, bearish, neutral non-volatile, and volatile strategies. In this chapter, we will cover at least one from each category.

The Advanced Strategies

The Call Backspread

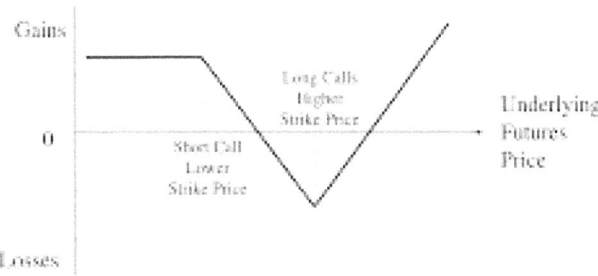

Call Backspread

The backspread is an options strategy that traders take up when they perceive that the market will be very volatile, though not 100% sure on the direction of the price. The stock's significant movement in the preferred direction earns them a big profit, but if it only moves a little, the trader earns a little profit. If the stock fails to move at all, the trader suffers a loss. Backspreads are also called reverse ratio spreads because they are designed to behave in the opposite direction of the ratio spreads.

When you are bullish on a particular stock, the backspread position you take is called the call ratio backspread, or simply, the call backspread. You enter this position when you buy a particular number of out-of-the-money call options (the kind whose strike price is more than stock value), and selling a smaller number of in-the-money call options (current stock price higher than the strike price). You have the liberty to choose the number of call options to sell or buy, but for now, let's only work with the case of a trader who buys 2 on-the-money call options then sells 1 in-the-money call option.

From buying the 2 call options and selling the 1 in-the-money call option, the trader has entered into what is called a credit position. This position allows the trader to earn a premium just by opening a call backspread. It happens when the trader buys the two call options, but since he is not willing to wait for the option to expire, he sells one option. However, even after the sale, the option owner still needs to buy back the option before it expires. These exchanges are what make taking this position quite risky.

If the stock price falls below the call option's strike price sold by the trader, then trader can allow the option to expire because, at this time, both strike prices are now meaningless. When this happens, the profit collected is the initial premium the trader made when he opened the position.

If the price of the stock rises high above the price of the strike price (in-the-money), but it is still below the strike price of the 2 calls, that the trader bought at the on-the-money price, the situation is no longer good. The 2 calls purchased on-the-money would become worthless, but the call the trader sold at the in-the-money strike price would still be worth something. It will need to be bought back before the contract expires.

Once the stock price has risen above the in-the-money strike price, the profits you can receive are limitless. The value of the in-the-money call rises, and even then, it must be bought back. The cost of purchasing the option, however, will be negated by the trader's possession of the 2 calls he bought at the in-the-money strike price. What's more, the two calls' value will be rising quickly, and the trader can sell them at a profit.

As a put, the backspread functions the same way, only in the opposite direction, in a bearish position.

Kindly remember that when it comes to the backspread position, you cannot allow your contracts to expire because the options you will have sold will need to be bought back to keep them from being exercised. As such, before you settle for the backspread, ensure that you have enough money to buy back the options in the event, the stock price fails to move.

The Synthetic Short Stock

The synthetic short stock is an options trading strategy that takes the form of buying or selling a stock, but with call or put options. It is taken up when the trader is bearish on a particular stock, and it involves buying a put option, then selling a call option with the same expiry date and at the same strike price.

In a typical situation where a trader only buys the basic put option, no profits would be realized until the stock price begins to fall under the strike price a bit. On the other hand, if the investor decides to invest in put options, he would have to pay the full premium, with the maximum possible loss being that premium.

In the case of the synthetic short stock, however, a trader can begin to enjoy some profits, once the stock price falls under the strike price, and the amount made after selling the corresponding call option makes up for the premium the trader spends buying the put option.

The advantages of the synthetic short stock strategy come with a big pay-off, unfortunately. The trader is now exposed to unlimited losses. For example, the more and more the value of the stock increases, the more the money the investor needs to buy back his call option before it expires. This makes taking this position very expensive, especially if the trader had made a faulty prediction concerning the likely direction of the stock.

The opposite of the synthetic short stock is the synthetic long stock. It behaves in a directly opposite behavior and is used by traders who feel bullish about their position to a stock.

That said, the synthetic stock strategies are thought to be excellent low-cost ways of dealing with basic options because their premiums are often offset once the trader sells the option under the opposite contract. However, this setup is seen to be almost similar to futures trading, and the thing with futures is that a wrong prediction could end up being too costly, just as we see with the synthetics.

The Long Butterfly Spread

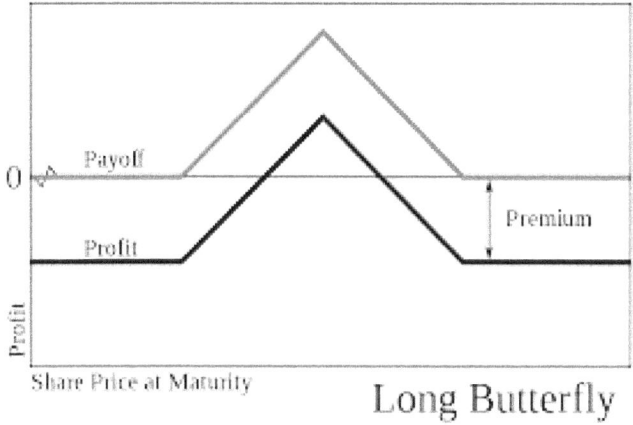

The Butterfly spread strategy is composed of 2 vertical spreads with a common strike price. The two spreads are the opening position where options are bought or sold, at 3 individual strike prices. These calls can be either calls or puts. The arrangement of the options makes the Butterfly spread a strategy that limits both profits and losses.

There is no difference between a Long Butterfly spread created with either calls or puts because, due to put-call parity, a Long Butterfly spread created out of put options behaves precisely like one created out of call options. Therefore, whichever you use, calls, or puts, you can create a Long Butterfly.

Take the example of a trader who purchases 1 in-the-money call option but sells 2 at-the-money call options, before purchasing another out-of-the-money call option. As you see, this strategy combines two opposing vertical spread options, which is how it got its name, the Butterfly Spread.

If you combine the profit profiles of the four call options mentioned above, you will realize that was the strike price to fall, the trader would only suffer limited losses. He would only lose the premium he paid trying to set up the entire butterfly arrangement. If the stock price were to climb very high, the losses would be limited too. However, if the stock price remained around the at-the-money strike price, the trader would receive some profit, but it too would be limited.

The Long Butterfly is thus a comfortably neutral strategy for when the market is experiencing low volatility because the trader will be making a correct bet, saying that the stock price would not be making much movement. Then he would receive the maximum profits, the limited ones we mentioned above.

Another advantage of the Butterfly strategy is that it is a low-risk approach. In case the stock climbs unexpectedly or crashes, the losses suffered will be limited.

The Short Butterfly strategy is just like the Long Butterfly strategy, but the roles are reversed. Its spreads are reversed, and it is taken up when the market is experiencing volatile shocks.

One keynote you ought to make regarding the Butterfly positions is that they involve three different strike prices, whether buying or selling options. To take it up, most brokers will ask you to pay 3 commissions to open the position, and you must pay 3 more commissions as you exit. Therefore, keep these commissions in mind when weighing the possibility of taking the Butterfly. See whether it will be a profitable strategy, given your circumstances. (Of course, the fees paid will vary from one broker to the next).

The Long Iron Condor

Iron Condors

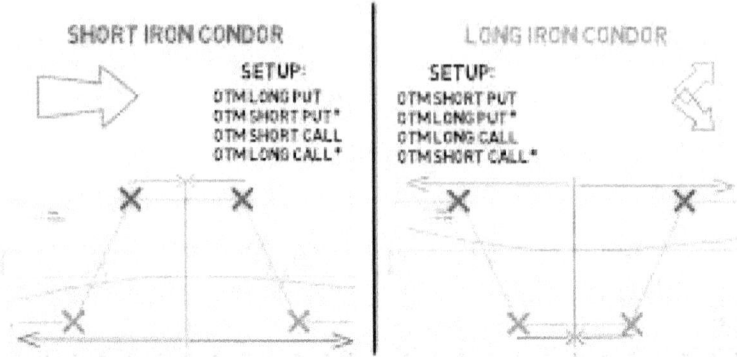

The Iron Condor strategies are an advanced strategy that, just like the Butterfly, uses two vertical spreads. The trader opens a call spread at a strike price higher than the current stock value of the underlying asset and opens a put spread too, at a strike price that is lower than the current stock value.

Of the Iron Condor strategies, the Long Iron Condor is the most popular, and it is also one of the most preferred advanced options buying strategies. Options trading instructors highly recommend it.

Using the Long Iron Condor strategy is similar to making a 'sure bet' although it leaves room for some modest profit and a few errors. The strategy is designed to be used on stocks that are not volatile, and those that maintain a neutral trading range. In addition, in case the stock price moves too much and the option reaches its expiration date, the losses resulting from this are very high, although limited.

The way to go about opening the Long Iron Condor position is by creating a bullish put spread and a bearish call spread. You create the call spread by selling 1 out-of-the-money call option and purchasing another call option whose out-of-the-money position is further along. You create the put by selling 1 out-of-the-money put option and then purchasing 1 put option that is further out-of-the-money. The spreads you will have created are credit spread, and once the position is opened, you can expect to reap some income from them.

Having this unique spreads together creates a target price range that falls between the inner out-of-the-money put strike price and the inner out-of-the-money call strike price. In the event the underlying stock price stays around this range by the time the expiry date comes, all four options will become worthless, and you get to keep the credit income you had at the start. If, however, the performance of the underlying stock becomes more volatile than you hoped and even gets out of the price range, you must close your in-the-money positions immediately. Unfortunately, doing this will reduce your profits and in the end, bring you a net loss.

In comparison to other neutral trading strategies, the Long Iron Condor stands out. If you compared it to similar strategies that deal with non-volatile stocks like the Strong Strangle and the Long Butterfly, you would note the differences. For example, if the price changes drastically, a trader using the Strong Strangle will suffer unlimited loss while a trader using the Long Iron Condor will only experience some limited maximum losses.

If the stock price remains at the same position without any movement, under the Long Butterfly, the trader will enjoy a maximum profit. However, the Long Iron Condor makes more room, with its more extensive price range, within which the trader can enjoy the maximum profit. This price range can be controlled too. If you make it narrower, you make room to receive more initial credit income, but this exposes you to the risk of having the stock price landing out of this range.

One significant disadvantage of the Long Iron Condor strategy is that it is made up of four individual options, and this could translate to higher commission costs, depending on the policies of your broker, in comparison to other strategies. What's more, the maximum loss potential that a trader stands to incur is often more than the initial credit income the trader placed when opening this position. These two factors are substantial, and they make the Long Iron Condor appear less profitable than people presume it to be. Therefore, before you take it up, it would serve you well to sit down and analyze all factors involved, weigh out the situation effectively, and see whether the strategy is appropriate for your trading goals. Do not forget to include the commission costs in your analysis.

The Short Iron Condor works in the opposite direction, and it is best suited for volatile stocks.

The Long Strangle

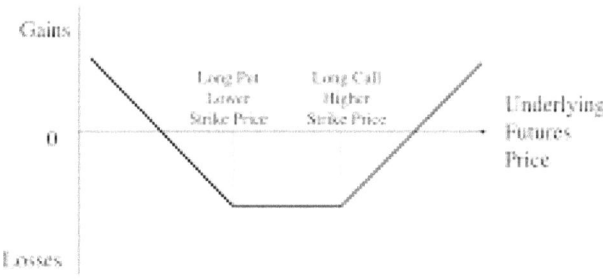

Strangle strategy options are strategies that thrive enable the trader's investments to thrive when the stock is volatile. The long strangle, for example, is the position a trader takes when anticipating high volatility in the underlying stock. The trader creates the Long Strangle position by purchasing 1 out-of-the-money call option, and 1 out-of-the-money put option. These options must share an expiration date.

Although the call option's stock price will be below the strike price, the call will not be worth anything, but once that stock price goes beyond the strike price, the call option will produce some profit. In the same way, the put option will be worthless so long as the stock price is above the option's strike price. However, once the strike price is higher than the stock price, the put option will begin to give some value.

When a trader brings together the two different profiles of the call and puts options, the result is the Long Strangle position. This strategy gives the trader the potential to make unlimited profits as the stock price climbs higher or falls lower. However, if the stock value stays within the confines of the two strike prices, both options will be rendered worthless, bringing a loss to the investment portfolio.

You ought to close your Long Strangle position before the expiry date of the options comes. You can do this by selling the option leg that has value and let the other option leg expire (expiry saves you some commission or fees charged when you transact). Therefore, if you realize that the stock has climbed, sell that call option and allow the put option to expire. If the stock price has fallen, expect the opposite. If the stock price remained stationary, you have to allow both options to expire, or if they have any time value left, you could sell them.

As we have mentioned, the Long Strangle is suitable for volatile stocks, those that you are sure will have dramatic climbs or falls in the future. This is a suitable strategy for when you are waiting for some big financial statement to be made, such as when a company is about to report on the performance of its stocks. If the performance has been good, the stock price will skyrocket, but if the performance was bad, the price would plummet. Other pieces of news that could cause volatility include the resolution of a lawsuit, the release of some research results, and a change of monetary or fiscal policy.

When it comes to strategy and execution, the Short Strangle is the Long Strangle is the exact opposite. The Short Strangle is best suited for stocks whose prices remain still and do not fluctuate. This makes it one of the neutral strategies that traders take up to reap profits out of very little if any, market activity.

The Call Ratio Spread

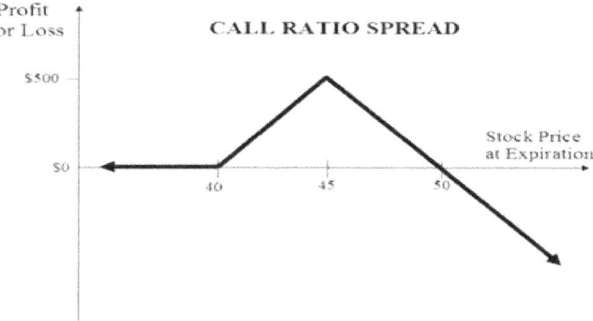

The ratio spread, also called the ratio vertical spread, is a strategy that is a variation of the vertical spread. It is a neutral spread that is built to be used in a neutral, non-volatile situation. With the word 'ratio' in its name, the strategy uses a 1-for-1 spread ration in which one option purchased is paired with another option sold. Traders set up this ratio spread by putting the options sold against options bought in a ratio. The ratio can have any numbers, but for the sake of understanding, let's work with a 2:1 ratio that represents 2 sold options put against 1 option bought.

As you can already tell, the Call Ratio Spread is a ratio spread created using call options. The trader buys 1 in-the-money call option and sells 2 at-the-money call options. The trader would be selling more options than he is buying, which essentially means that the seller is giving naked or uncovered options. A naked-options situation always brings with it many risks, and some brokers do not like to do business with traders dealing with uncovered options unless you demonstrate to them that you have adequate experience trading options.

The Call Ratio Spread strategy has some advantages, though. One of them is that the initial cost of opening this position is almost negligible, and the trader might even find himself earning some money. The second advantage is that the cost of the in-the-money call option is more than that of an at-the-money call option. Therefore, the cash you spend buying the 1 in-the-money call option will be offset by the premium you get when you sell 2 at-the-money calls.

Now that this strategy allows you to earn some income as you set things up, it has also earned the name Ratio Credit Spread.

At the time of expiry, in the event the value of the underlying stock has fallen below the in-the-money strike price, the three options become worthless, and the trader does not make any additional losses or profits. If the stock value has gone up high than the in-the-money strike price, the seller can sell the in-the-money call option he bought previously.

Your income increases as the stock value gets closer to the strike price of the call option at-the-money. If the stock value goes higher than the strike price of the call option at-the-money, you now will need to purchase back the 2 at-the-money call options that you had sold previously. This will cause you to suffer larger and larger losses as you try to buy back your two options, with only the premium from the 1 in-the-money option remaining to offset your losses.

A trader who has taken up the Ratio Credit Spread strategy is only able to realize a maximum profit when the stock value ends up at the position next to the strike price of the at-the-money call options. From there, the trader will sell the call option in-the-money for the maximum amount possible, while allowing the at-the-money calls to expire and become worthless. However, as the stock price rises, the losses increase too.

As such, the Call Ratio Spread strategy is suitable for neutral situations, where the stocks are non-volatile. If the stock value goes down, the trader experiences limited to no losses, but if the stock value has risen up, the trader suffers limited losses.

The Call Ratio Spread is similar to its counterpart, the Put Ratio Spread, only that the latter is constructed using put options rather than with call options. The Ratio Spread is also identical to the Butterfly and the Iron Condor that are also used when handling non-volatile stocks. The only difference is that the Ratio Spread allows for the recurrence of unlimited losses if the underlying stock is too volatile. However, the fact that the Ratio Spread only includes a few options limits the extents of the risks. In addition, there are fewer commissions because there are fewer positions to open and close.

Chapter 10: Technical Indicators

Depending on the type of security and the trading style a trader is handling, there many technical indicators in the market. However, this chapter discusses the most popular and most useful technical indicators for an options trader.

Generally, technical indicators are taken up in the short-term, and the choice of an indicator depends on the direction the price takes the range by which it moves, and the duration the price goes in a particular direction.

Another factor to remember is that the holding period of your options matters because options are subject to time decay. Options have time limits by which the positions must be executed, unlike other investments like stocks in which a trader can hold a position indefinitely. Since timing is critical, you will see that momentum indicators, the kind that is meant to show the options that are oversold or overbought, are popular among traders.

Technical Indicators Used in Options Trading

Bollinger Bands

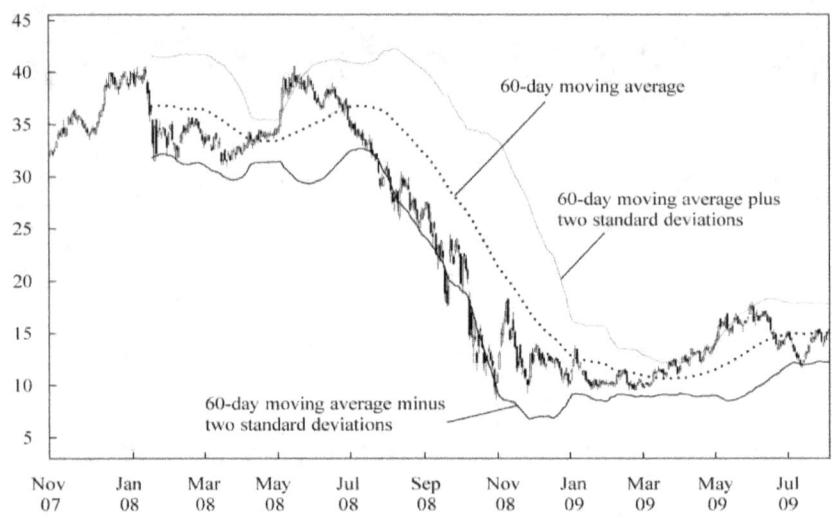

Bollinger Bands is an indicator that shows the volatility of options. It is taken up to indicate the high and the low volatility levels on a price chart. This indicator cannot be used on its own; traders use it to complement oscillator-type, trend-following indicators, and this makes their trading activities more effective. For example, when there is little or no market activity, it is often difficult to predict the direction the price will take in the future, but with Bollinger Bands, traders can foretell the prevalent market phase.

Bollinger Bands are made up of a moving average and two lines that are extrapolated from the two standard deviations on whichever side of the central moving average. The two lines you extrapolate make up the band. If the band is narrow, the market is quiet, and if the band is wide, the market is loud. Therefore, the Bollinger Band can be used both in a trending and a ranging market.

When the market is trending, use the Bollinger Squeeze to mark your trade entry so that you can catch breakouts early enough. The Bollinger Squeeze is when the bands are close together, it appears like they are squeezing. The squeeze is a sign that a breakout is close by, although it will not tell you anything about the direction the price is likely to go.

The price movement is likely to continue in its downward trend if you see the candles breakout below the bottom band. The candles breaking out above the top band indicate an uptrend.

When the market is ranging, let the Bollinger Bounce guide you. During the bounce, the price bounces from one side of the band to the next but continuously goes back to the stirring average, in a sort of regression to the mean. Naturally, the value will get back to the average with time.

In a situation where the market is ranging, the bands become resistance and support levels, and if the value reaches the top of the band, the trader needs to place a stop-loss slightly above the band to keep it from breaking out. The price ought to revert to the average or the bottom band, and there, the trader can take profits.

In summary, the Bollinger Bounce in a ranging market indicates that the price will go back to the mean, and in a trending market, the Bollinger Squeeze indicates that the price is about to break out, although it does not indicate the direction the price is likely to take.

Relative Strength Index (RSI)

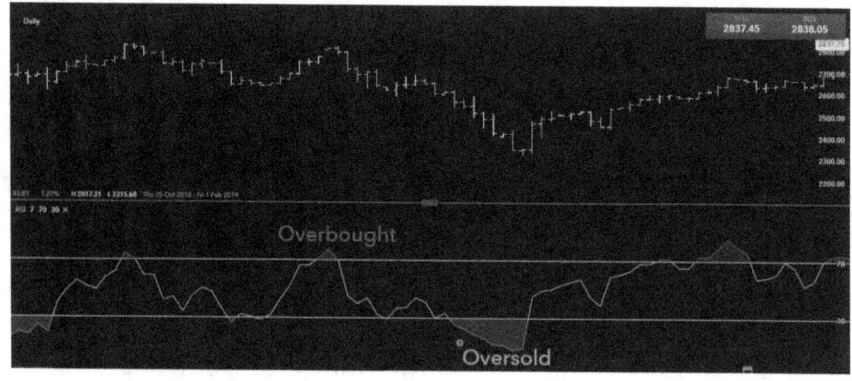

The RSI is an indication of the momentum, giving buy or sell signals to the trader. This indicator works under very simple logic: when the underlying asset is oversold, its price will be lower than what would be considered normal. An oversold asset is most likely to appreciate in the nearby future. If the underlying asset is overbought, the price will be higher than it usually should be, and it is expected to deflate in the near future. Therefore, with the RSI, you will differentiate the oversold and the overbought positions.

The setup of the RSI is relatively simple also. Usually, the indicator is plotted on a different scale, and a single line, with a scale ranging from 0 to 100, is used to identify the oversold and the overbought market conditions. If the readings are beyond 70, that is an oversold market, and if the evaluations are below 30, know that the market is oversold.

The idea behind using the RSI is to correctly identify the tops and bottoms so that the trader moves into the market just when a trend is reversing. The early entry allows the trader to take advantage of the entire market move before another cycle begins.

To confirm trend formations, you could also use the RSI. If the RSI is above the level of 50-marks, the market will be in an uptrend, and if the line is below the level of 50-marks, the market will be on a downtrend. A risk-averse trader should probably wait for trend confirmation before entering a position. However, he may not make as much as he would, had he moved in before the trend began.

You see, trading always involves a trade-off of two things. You stand to make lots of profit if you get into a trend early, but unfortunately, you stand to make mistakes much more often, and you could end up losing your trading capital. On the other hand, you might be able to wait to confirm the trend but only make conservative profits. However, when you wait, you increase your chances of being right most times. It all depends on your disposition to risk.

Ichimoku Kinko Hyo

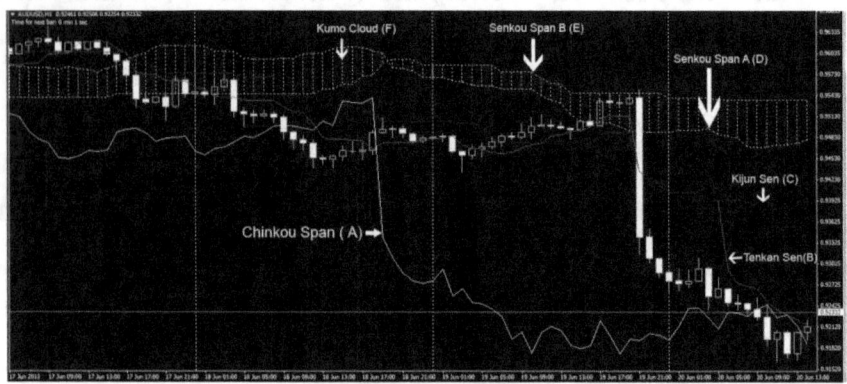

The Ichimoku Kinko Hyo, also called the Ichimoku Cloud, is a momentum indicator that shows future price momentum and indicates areas that are likely to provide support or resistance in the future. By its name and description, in addition to the number of lines that are plotted, it may appear like a complex indicator, but it really isn't.

Here's what each of the lines on the graph means:
- The green line called the lagging line or the Chikou Span is the closing price of the day plotted 26 periods behind.

- The red line called the turning line, or the Tenkan-Sen is one that is derived by getting the average of the highest highs and the lowest lows for the last 9 periods.

- The blue line, called the Kijun-Sen, the baseline, or the standard line, is a line determined by calculating the average of the lowest low and the highest high for the last 26 periods.

- There also is a red or green band called the Senkou Span. Its first line is computed by finding the median if the Kijun-Sen and the Tenkan-Sen, plotted 26 periods ahead. Its second line is calculated by averaging the lowest low and the highest high over the last 52 periods, but it is plotted 26 periods ahead.

The lines described above, it would seem, are difficult to translate when trading. However, that is not the case. The Senkou Span takes the role of offering dynamic resistance and support because if the prices go above the Senkou span, the top of the line will act as the first support point while the bottommost of the line will be the second support point. If the values fall under the Senkou span, its bottom line becomes the first resistance point while the top line becomes the second resistance point.

Traders use the Kijun-Sen to confirm trends. If the price breaks out at a point above the Kijun-Sen, the price will likely even go further up. In the same way, if the price drops below the line, it will unmistakably go lower.

The Tenkan-Sen is another line used to confirm trends. You will know that the market is trending when you see the line moving up and down. If it changes sideways, understand that the market is fluctuating. Take note that this red line indicates the price trend.

The Chikou Span, the colored-green one, is plotted 26 periods following the present period. It indicates trends of all sorts. Whenever this line crosses the price headed to the top from the bottom, know that the price will likely follow and go up. If the line crosses the price from up headed downwards, the price is likely to follow that direction too and will go from up to down.

As you see, this indicator shows quite a lot of information about a trade; you only have to recall what each line means. If you mixed up the colors, you could make a mistake and end up losing your investment, bringing down your portfolio.

Simple Moving Average (SMA)

This indicator is great for assessing the trend prevailing. There will be times when the direction a trend is taking will not be so obvious. The span a trend takes to complete also varies (there are medium-term and long-term trends). In cases like this, the SMA helps the trader to understand the market trends.

Traders can also combine the SMA with other indicators to get some clarity on some buy and sell signals.

The Moving Average Convergence Divergence (MACD)

This is a trend indicator, and like its counterpart, the Ichimoku Cloud, it has many parts to take note of. First, note that it is comprised of a slow line, a fast line, and a histogram. Understanding how they work can be confusing, so be attentive.

The inputs you need for this indicator are a slower moving average (MA-slow), a faster-moving average (MA-fast), a number that additionally defines the period of the third moving average, the MA-period.

The fast line of the MACD is a moving of the moving average of the difference among the fast-moving average and the slower-moving average (MA-fast – MA-slow). On the other hand, the

MACD slow line is a moving average of the MACD fast line. The number of periods for which it moves is determined by the MA-period.

The final component, the histogram, is designed to indicate the difference between the fast and the slow lines of the MACD.

Let's look at an example to help you understand what I mean. Suppose to have a "12, 26, 9" MACD, which is a typical default setting, you will interpret it as follows: the first line will be the moving average among the 12-period and the 26-period moving averages. The slow line is the one in the 9-period moving average of the fast line. The histogram is the difference between the MACD lines.

Now that you understand that, let's now head on to explaining what the convergence and divergence are about. You will see that during plotting, the histogram and the moving averages are placed on separate charts and that the lines keep crossing over. As the difference between them continues to get smaller, the lines continue to get closer to each other. That is what we call convergence. If the difference is getting bigger and the lines are drawing further apart, they are diverging. Simple, right? When using the MACD indicator, take note of the distances and the tendencies of these lines.

Whenever a new trend is coming up in the market, the MACD lines converge, and when the trend reverses, they cross over and then begin to diverge. At the crossover point, the histogram disappears due to the dissimilarity among the fast and the slow lines will be zero.

One fact to have at the back of your mind is that the MACD indicator is made up of moving averages or other moving averages. As such, it tends to lag overdue the value a lot, making it a not-so-effective indicator for detecting trends early on. However, it is one of the best indicators for confirming trends.

Stochastic Indicator

This is the momentum indicator. It is aiding in helping determine the point at which a trend could end. The trader could use the end of a trend to pick an entry point so that he can get into the next trend at the very beginning. Just like the RSI indicator, it is used when the underlying stock or other asset has been oversold and overbought.

The stochastic indicator is made up of two lines, plotted on different charts. Once the lines are plotted above 80, it means that the market is oversold, there is possible to a downward trend. If the stochastic lines are plotted below 20, it means that the market is overbought, that there's about to be an uptrend.

As you try to get into trades early, be on the lookout because there are many fakeouts in the market. To prevent too much loss in the case, the market does not go in the predicted direction, install stop-losses.

Therefore, let the stochastic indicator only give you a clue of where the market is most likely to go; don't base the entire investment on it. Take on various risk management practices to keep your portfolio safe.

Money Flow Index (MFI)

Is the momentum indicator. It works by bringing together data regarding the price and volume of the underlying asset. Some investors call it the weighted-volume RSI.

The MFI measures how money is flowing in and out of an asset over a specified period, usually 14 days. The outcome it gives indicates the trading pressure in regards to the asset being traded. A reading beyond 80, just as with other indicators, is a sign that the asset is oversold whereas an analysis below 20 means that the security is overbought.

Since the MFI indicator deals with volume data, best suitable for stock-based options as against to index-based options, particularly the long-duration kind. Whenever the MFI moves in the direction reverse to that of the stock value, know that a trend change is impending.

Open Interest (OI)

The Open Interest is an indicator of the unsettled or open contracts in options trading. It does not indicate any specific information about where a trend is heading, but it does offer information about the strong point of the trend you are observing.

An increasing open interest is a sign that there is a new capital inflow, and this shows that the existing trend is sustainable. A declining open interest shows that the trend is weakening.

Options traders who seek to benefit from short-term trends and movements should take in the following scenarios:

- If the price is rising and the open interest is rising, the market or the security is strong.

- If the price is rising, but the open interest is falling, the market or the security is weakening

- If the price is falling, but the open interest is rising, the market or security is weakening

- If the price is falling and the open interest is falling, the market or security is strengthening.

Intraday Momentum Index (IMI)

This is an excellent indicator that high-frequency options traders use to wager on the price moves of the day. The indicator brings together the RSI and intraday candlesticks, creating a suitable range, like that of the RSI, for intraday trading; hence, it can accurately indicate what has been oversold and what has been overbought.

Using the IMI, an options trader will be able to take note of possible chances that could help him to initiate a bullish trade in a market that is trending upwards at an intraday correction. The trader is also able to initiate a bearish trade in a market whose trend is headed downwards at an intraday price bump.

Traders compute the IMI by finding the sum of up days and dividing it by the sum of up days plus the sum of down days (Sum of up / (Sum of up days + Sum of down days). The result is then multiplied by 100. The trader has the liberty to choose the number of days from which to look, but the most commonly used number is 14 days.

Just as when you use the RSI if the result goes beyond 70, the stock or other asset is considered overbought, if the digit is less than 30, the stock is oversold.

Chapter 11: Some Case Studies on Options Trading

Case studies allow traders to have a clearer understanding of the options strategies and the outcomes to expect so that they can avoid the errors or take up the same steps that the traders in the case study used. Here are a few case studies to provide you with a practical approach to options trading:

Case Study #1

This is a study of a metal works company that is concerned about the rising prices of one of its critical inputs, steel. The current market price of the steel is $400 per ton, but the manufacturer is afraid that the price could rise and get to more than $500 per ton.

To remedy the situation, the investor decided to buy a call option at $500 per ton. The call option strike price is equivalent to the forecast threshold that the investor is worried about.

Once he purchases the call option, the investor pays a premium to the writer of the option so that if the market price does not go above the $500 per ton, the option will expire out-of-the-money. If this happens, the investor will not experience too much loss when the option expires because he will still be able to buy his steel below the $500 threshold. The only loss he will incur is the premium he paid to the writer of the option.

In the event the market price exceeds $500 per ton, the option will expire in-the-money, and the option holder will make a profit from it. For example, if the price goes as high as $550 per pound of steel, the investor will exercise his option and will purchase a ton of steel at $500, from the option writer. He makes a profit of his savings, less the premium he paid. In case the premium was $10, the profit will be $40. This is found by ($550 -$500) - $10. Hence, the investor will be protected against the steel price going above $500 per ton.

In this example, the call option serves as a hedge against the changes in the steel market. The call option's interactions remain the same despite the changes in the market. In the investor's case above, it is clear that the out-of-money option puts a limit to the downside to the premium paid on the option,

$10. All market prices will experience a downside up to, and including, premium and the strike price. However, once the market price exceeds the sum of the premium and the strike price, the investor will enjoy a profit. Luckily, the profit or the upside is unlimited.

In this example, the option purchased will have been a successful hedge against an anticipated rise in the price of steel. The call option limits the downside to the price of the premium but maintains an open door to the profits through the unlimited upside.

Case Study #2

Here's a case study borrowed from the Terry Tips blog.

Costco had begun trading in 2015 at $141.87, and at that time, Terry Tips' portfolio, one that uses COST as the underlying asset, was valued at $6223. Had this money been devoted, it would have produced 43.8 shares or roughly 44 shares of the stock.

Early in that year, the price rose steadily but fell from a $153 high to a $135 low within the first week of September. By the end of that month, the stock was now trading at $3 higher than it had traded when the year began.

If you were to compare the value of the 44 COST shares and the current value of the Terry Tips portfolio had it traded options in that same period, the situation could have been as follows:

When the stock fell a little in January, the value of the portfolio could the value of the portfolio followed and fell by an even more considerable amount. However, as the value of the stock recovered, the portfolio outdid it again and outperformed on the upside also.

Over the nine months between January and September, investing in stocks could only have produced returns of $1.20 per share, which means that for the 44 shares, the investor would have received $52.80. The stock obtained $2.70 per share above the 9-months that the 44 shares would have increased their worth by $118.80 compared to their value at the beginning of the year. This increase translates to a $171.60 net gain, adding the $52.80 dividends paid out. The net gain represents a 1.2% gain in the value of the stocks in 9 months.

Above the equal period, the definite COST options portfolio had risen in value to $12,900 from $6,223, a net gain of $6,667, which represents a 107% increased value.

Looking at the trading strategy used, Terry Tips owned seven calls, all of which expired in April, and two others that would extend until July. They had also sold 8 calls that expired on

January 15, of which 3 had a strike price just under the stock value, while the remaining 5 were somewhat out-of-the-money. The company also have 1 long uncovered call against, that they could have sold a short-term call; nevertheless, they thought it better to maintain a higher net delta. With that portfolio, and with different options positions, Terry Tips owned about 218 shares of stock, which does not compare to directly owning 44 shares.

By the end of the nine months, on September 25, all the long calls had been pushed to January to April of the next year, 2016, and the company still held a few put positions. In May, when the COST shares were selling at $144, the company had sold a bullish credit put spread. (It had bought October-15 135 puts but sold October-15 140 puts). Terry Tips figured that if the price were above $140 at the time when the puts expire on October 16, the puts would have been rendered worthless, and the company would have 51% on the quantity it had risked when it sold its spread in May.

Halfway through 2015, Terry Tips decided to switch tactics and change how it traded its portfolio. By now, they were now short some weekly options for numerous dissimilar series. Therefore, individual week, when some calls would expire, Terry Tips would repurchase them on a Friday, typically, and then sell the new ones, which would have a four-week time limit.

The company was careful to pick out only the strikes that would balance out its risk profile by carefully weighing its portfolio. This also gave them the opportunity to tweak its investment profile each week, and to make small changes, rather than waiting to make some grand alterations at the end of the month when the options expired. The company credits its superior performance while managing the profile to its style of trading, saying that it would not have been possible had the company not taken up the weekly options.

At the end of every week, on Friday, the company would create a risk-profile graph so that it would act as the guide in helping them choose the strike prices to use when it buys back the expiring weekly options to change them with new short calls whose expiry was further out.

The value gained from trading options does not compare to one gained trading stocks. With a starting value of $6,223, the company realized a 107% portfolio gain, even higher than the income the investors started with. A person who chose to safely invest in stocks by buying COST shares would only have gained $172, 1.2% of his portfolio. The options portfolio outperformed the gains from the stocks so many times over.

The Terry Tips example clearly illustrates, beyond all doubt, that when options strategies are correctly executed, they can out-perform the direct shares purchase. Indeed, it is much easier to buy stock, and it involves less risk, but although trading options is demanding and involves much more risks, it is sure worth investing it because, with attention and time, it performs many times better than shares.

Case Study #3

Let's see how this second case compares to the COST investment example (both made by Terry Tips).

Terry Tips decided to invest in Starbucks because its stock had been doing so well, particularly in the first 9 months of the year 2015. At the beginning of the year, the stock started at $81.44 then rose steadily to $98 before the two for one stock split in early April. By the end of the ninth month, September, the stock was trading at $57.99, which got to $115.98 as the pre-split price. Starbucks paid three $.16 dividend then paid another $0.48 to the total adding up to a total of $35.02, which translates to a 43% gain in the 9 months.

Terry Tips started the year by investing $6032 and invested in Starbucks options. Had they purchased the shares themselves, at $81.44 per share, the company would only have afforded to purchase 74 shares. In only 9 months, the portfolio would have procured $11,768 or 195% in value.

Unfortunately, Terry Tips' portfolio did not gain much because they had also invested an equal amount with the Keurig Green Mountain (GMCR), another coffer company. Over the same period, the GMCR portfolio lost $8905 because the stock value fell from $130 to $50s. However, the company did drop GMCR stock in August, and the company added FB to its portfolio, now dealing with FB and Starbucks stock, but in separate portfolios.

The portfolio established at the beginning of the year reached $10,604, and by the end of the nine months, it had gone up to $12,708. The value increase was $2182, which is 20.5%. This was a small, though not bad, value gain over the 9 months, considering that the market had fallen by 6.7%. However, this does not compare to the 195% the company would have enjoyed had it stuck to the Starbucks investment alone.

The three case studies described above are enough proof that if options strategies are correctly executed, they can outright outperform the direct bought of shares, by numerous times over. Absolutely, it's safe, uncomplicated, and less demanding to choose to invest in the stock, but if you are willing to put in the work, by giving your portfolio the time, the attention, and the research it demands. You will end up earning profits of 195% instead of a mere 43%, or 107%, rather than 1.2% with the same investment, using the same stock.

If you wish to take up options trading but don't have the time or the knowledge you would require to run a self-directed options trading account, opt for the auto-trade services that most brokers offer. The trades will be made automatically for you, and although you might have to pay some commission, it doesn't compare to getting the 1.2% returns you would get investing in stocks under the buy-and-hold setup.

Chapter 12: Strategies to Apply Easily to Options Trading

There are many options trading strategies available, and each comes with the promise of increasing returns, protecting what you got by minimizing risks, or both. With only a clear understanding of how the strategies work, potential traders can learn how to take advantage of the opportunities that come up.

Below is a discussion of some of the strategies investors can take up:

Options Trading Strategies

The Long Call

The long call is the choice options trading strategy is popular among aggressive investors who feel very bullish about an index or a stock. When a trader is feeling bullish, he expects that the stock price will go beyond the strike price at the time of expiration.

The advantage of taking up this strategy is that the upside, the profits side, is uncapped so that when the stock price goes up, the trader can make profits as far as the stock price can go.

Theoretically, the upside is infinite, and if the stock continually rises before expiration, the call continues to climb also. This one advantage makes long calls one of the most popular to bet on the stock price.

Let's look at a sample. If a particular underlying stock, Y, is exchange at $15 per share and its call, at the strike price of $15 that expires in four months is trading at $2, your contract (typically of 100 shares) will cost you $200. If the shares go up by $2, the share price will be $17. As such, for every change in value above $15, the options contract will increase in value by $200. If the value drops under the $15 strike price, the options contract will be worthless.

The downside of the long call is the complete loss of your investment. If the stock closes under the strike price, the call will become useless, and the trader will lose the premium that he paid when purchasing the option.

Seeing that the risk can be quite significant, opt to take up the long call strategy only when you expect that the price of the stock will rise significantly within the stipulated time limit. If the rise only rises a little bit above the strike price, the option will still be in-the-money, but it is less likely to return the premiums you have paid. You will only experience loss.

The Long Put Strategy

The long put strategy is quite different from the long call. The first thing you need to note about their differences is that buying a call is the opposite of buying a put. When you are bearish about a stock, you buy the put option, but when you are bullish, you purchase the call option. The put option allows the buyer the right to sell stock to the put seller at a predetermined price, and this limits his risks. As such, the long put is a bearish strategy, and traders invest in it to take advantage of the falling market.

Suppose stock Y is trading at $10 per share, and its accompanying options have a $10 strike price, is retailing at $1, and expiring in four months. For every dollar decline in price, the $10 put will increase in value. Above $11, the put will expire, become worthless, and the trader will have lost his $100 premium.

Your long put's upside is similar to that of holding a long call: the upside is not capped, and the value of the option premium can increase many times over. However, the upside is not theoretically unlimited because the stock can never go below zero. As you see, the long put presents an exciting way to take on the decline of the stock, and they tend to be safer than shorting a stock.

The advantage of the long put is that its downside is capped at the $100 premium you paid, and this only happens when the stock closes at a price above the strike price. If this happens, your put option immediately expires, and you remain with nothing.

Therefore, use the long put strategy when you expect that the value of the stock will drop to heights significantly lesser than the strike price before the time limit is up. Be careful, though, because if your prediction is not as accurate and the price falls just slightly lower than the strike price, although it will be in-the-money, you could end up losing your premium altogether.

The Short Call

In a case where a trader anticipates that the stock price will rise in the future, the trader opts for the long call strategy. However, when the trader predicts that the value of the underlying stock will fall, the trader will take up the short call strategy. The short call strategy is also called the Short Naked Call strategy because the investor does not hold any underlying stock when he is shorting.

The investor begins to sell call options because he or she is bearish about a particular index or stock, and he expects the prices to fall later. The short call is one position that offers minimal chances of making profits, and the situation could quickly turn around so that the investor begins to suffer losses, in the event the underlying price begins to increase instead of decreasing.

Although the short call strategy is easily implemented, it can get quite risky, mainly because it exposes the seller of the call option to unlimited risks.

The Short Put Strategy

Just as you would expect, the short put strategy is the exact opposite of the long put strategy. However, in this case, the trader sells his put because he anticipates that the stock price will rise before the set time limit expires. In exchange for the put option, the trader gets a cash premium, and this is the best possible outcome a short put can have. If the stock closes at a price lower than the strike price, the options trader must now buy it at the strike price.

An example might make it easier to see how the short put strategy is used. Let's say a specific stock, stock K has its shares selling at $10 each, its options are trading at $1, and that the option expires in the next four months. Taking into account the fact that an options contract typically holds 100 shares, the contract will attract a premium of $100.

In the event the option breaks even at $9, under the short put strategy, the short put will cost the trader $100 per dollar decline in value. If the value goes above the strike price, say, $11, the seller will earn a clean $100 premium.

The upside of the short put does not go above the premium the seller received, in this case, the $100. As such, the maximum returns the seller can enjoy under the short put is the amount that the buyer presents upfront.

The downside, on the other hand, is the total value of the underlying stock, a lesser amount of the premium the seller has collected. However, this would only happen if the value of the stock got to zero. In the example above, the trader would be asked to buy stock worth $1000 ($10 * 100 shares). However, the premium the trader would receive would offset the $100 premium the seller received, causing the total loss to be $900 ($1000 - $100).

The short put strategy is best taken up when the seller expects the stock to rise in value, high beyond the strike price, by the time it expires. The stock only needs to be above or just around the strike price for the option to lose its value. If that happened, the seller would keep the entire premium received. That said, your broker will still be concerned to see whether your account holds enough equity to buy the stock if the opportunity to do so comes up. If the put closes while still in-the-money, the money will be left in your trading account.

The Long Straddle Strategy

The long straddle strategy is also called the 'straddle' or the 'buy straddle' strategy. It is one of the neutral options trading strategies, and it involves simultaneously buying a call and put option of the same underlying stock. Since the positions are long in for both the put and the call, the strike price and the expiration date of the options are the same. This strategy can achieve large profits, whichever direction the price shifts to because the trader has covered both sides. However, just like the other positions, the move the price makes must be strong, for the trader to enjoy any significant progress.

The investor buys the long straddle when he thinks that the underlying stock or index will have some significant volatility in the near future. Any risk that the investor experiences is limited to the initial premium paid.

The Short Straddle Strategy

The short straddle strategy is the exact opposite of the long straddle strategy. An investor takes up the short straddle strategy when he or she perceives that there will not be much movement in the market in the coming days. For this reason, the investor sells a put and a call option of the same stock or index. The pair, the put, and call often share the strike price and the maturity date, just like those of the long straddle.

The result is that selling the two options generates a net income for the seller. If the underlying stock or index does not make much movement in either direction, the investor keeps the premium, and neither of the two options is exercised.

Unfortunately, this strategy exposes the investor to unlimited risk while the reward is limited to the premium the investor will receive for the options sold. If the stock happens to move significantly, either upwards or downwards, the investor stands to lose a significant amount. Since this is a risky strategy, investors should exercise caution before adopting it by studying the market hard to ensure that their predictions are right. The strategy should only be adopted once the trader is sure that the expected volatility in the market will be limited.

The Married Put Strategy

The married put strategy is similar to the long put strategy, only that it has a twist. For this one, the trader already owns stock but goes ahead to buy a put of that same underlying stock. This strategy is done to hedge the existing stock in a case where the trader expects that the stock price will go up but still wants to have some form of insurance, just in case the stock falls. If the stock price were to fall, the long put would offset the loss.

Theoretically, the married put's upside is uncapped, for as long as the stock continues to rise. Taking this strategy puts the trader at a hedge position, having paid the premium as insurance to allow the stock to rise, while still limiting how far it goes to the downside.

The married put's downside, therefore, is the value of the premium paid, and as the value of the stock goes down, the value of the put itself increases, covering the fall in price. For this reason, the options trader only loses what it costs to buy the option rather than the more significant value of the stocks he owns.

The best time to take up the married put option is when the trader expects that the price of his stock will rise significantly before the options' expiry date, but also understands that there is a slim chance that the price could fall dramatically. With the married stock, you get the satisfaction of holding the stock that comes with enjoying its upside when it rises, but still be covered in case of a substantial loss, when the stock falls.

Traders buy the married put when they expect news and events in the future that could drive the cost of their stock upwards or downwards but still desires to be covered.

The Covered Call Strategy

When it comes to dealing with calls, one of the best strategies is to go ahead and buy a naked call option. You could also structure a buy-write or a basic covered call.

The covered call is quite widespread among traders since it helps to generate income while reducing the risks associated with the long stock. However, to do this, you must be willing to trade your shares as the predetermined price at the strike price of the short call. Therefore, to use this strategy, you must first get into the market, purchase the underlying stock as a normal stock investor would, and then write a call option on those same shares.

E.g., a call option on a stock that carries 100 shares in each call option. To cover the call, you must sell 1 call option against the 100 shares of stock that you have purchased. If the stock you have purchased skyrockets in price, your short call will be covered by the long stock position you have taken. This is the reason it is called a covered call.

Traders take up the covered call strategy when they hold a short-term position in the stock, and a neutral opinion on the direction the price of the stock is headed. The investor could be looking to sell the call, get the premium and gain some income, or they could be making an effort to protect their stock against a possible decline of the value of the underlying stock.

The Protective Collar Strategy

The protective collar strategy is the one in which traders purchase out-of-the-money put options and at the same time, write an out-of-the-money call option of the same underlying asset, and with a similar expiration date. It is a mix of a long put and a covered call.

The combination creates a neutral setup that protects the trader in case the stock falls, but on the other hand, it gives the investor the responsibility of selling his long stock at the short call strike price. This is not too bad for the investor because he will have experienced the benefits of holding the underlying shares.

Investors use the protective collar when in a long position, and the stock they are holding has had some substantive gains. The stock and options combination allows the investor to enjoy downside protection through the long put so that he or she locks in the profit, while at the same time, getting the pleasure of selling his shares at a high price.

Suppose an investor is long on some Company Y shares, 100 shares at $50, and the value of the shares rises to $100, the investor will create a protective collar by selling one call at $105, and simultaneously buying another at $95. As such, the trader will be protected below the $95, but this is a trade-off with the obligation to sell his shares at $105.

There is an infinite number of strategies that investors can take up to trade options. However, what will be of help to you, in the long run, is to approach the market with a lot of caution, to be systematic and to be probability-minded. Whichever strategy you take up, ensure that you have done your homework first by gaining a sound knowledge of the market and being conscious of the goal you intend to achieve. You must choose the most suited strategy for the market condition you are in.

While the risks involved might appear to be quite significant, the options trading strategies with a risk limit will control the risk to which the trader is exposed. As such, even the risk-averse traders can invest in options to increase their overall returns, protect their current stocks, and reap other benefits that options have to offer. However, as we have pointed out earlier, it helps to understand all the upside and the downside of each investment strategy before you take it up so that you are fully aware of what you stand to lose if the market does not go your way, and what you stand to gain if it does.

Description

The resources people find on the internet in the form of articles and research papers are excellent and informative, but the problem with that kind of knowledge is its lack of arrangement. Most of these resources will give you distorted information because however, you concentrate, you will find something that will distract you. As you are reading about options, you will find an attached article on cooking styles, and as you read on, you will find a funny cat video or an ad. Once you are on that trail, there is no going back. It is no wonder the greatest minds of our time insist on books, not videos or articles. They say that distorted knowledge leads to a distorted mind. It is a joy to bring you an ordered, well-written book on options and options trading.

Options Trading Strategies: Advanced Guide with All the Latest Winning Strategies, Practical Tips, and Suggestions That Will Make the Difference in Your Trading. Start Generating Income Now is designed to equip you with the latest and most practical knowledge on tips, techniques, and strategies that will get you more informed and equipped to trade efficiently.

You see, almost everyone wants to have multiple streams of income. We read about it in motivational books. We also have motivational speakers pounding information into our heads about how important it is to begin projects that will help us to raise both passive and active income-generating projects and looking at various industries; we can agree that the financial market is one of the most lucrative.

Instead of marching forth and doing something, our journey towards self-improvement ends with us nodding our heads and scribbling some illegible words on our notepads. Well, this ends today because I am here to remind us of one incredibly lucrative venture: options trading. Through this reading, I take you back to the basics of options and options trading strategies, starting from the basics and building up to advanced knowledge.

In this book, you will find:

- Basic training on options and options trading
- Information on various commissions, fees, and the effects of slippage
- The most informative discussion on about brokers and trading platforms, along with advice on how to find the best ones
- An identification of risks involved in trading and techniques you can use to limit your risk exposure
- Training on how you can develop your own trading strategy

- The most explicit instructions on how to use technical indicators to analyze your trade positions
- The most insightful discussion of several basic options trading strategies
- A comprehensive review of several advanced options trading strategies
- The most in-depth assessment of some case studies that demonstrate the effectiveness of options as a trading tool in comparison to other techniques

Conclusion

Thank you for making it through to the end of *Options Trading Strategies: Advanced Guide with All the Latest Winning Strategies, Practical Tips and Suggestions That Will Make the Difference in Your Trading. Start Generating Income Now,* let's hope it was informative and able to provide you with all of the tools you need to achieve your goals, whatever they may be.

With all the myths debunked and all the misinformation corrected, I am confident that you feel more optimistic and convinced that options' trading is the way to go. It is surprising to see that with rich resources like this, not many people take up this lucrative trading business. However, it is said that success is the path less traveled, and I am glad you are on it.

Writing this book was a revelation for me, too. I realized that there exist many hidden pockets of knowledge I had not known about. It is incredible how, in the course of pass knowledge to you, I ended up learning a lesson or two myself.

It is my sincere hope that through this book, you have learned and increased your knowledge of options and how they are traded. You have also learned about the types of options, the risks involved in trading, and the techniques you can utilize to manage that risk. You also know how to use technical signals and indicators to interpret trends in the financial market. You also now understand basic and advanced trading strategies.

The next step is to take the bull by its horns. Do not waste your knowledge. If you are new to options trading, go on and make plans to start trading soon. If you have been trading, take up the tips and techniques, and implement them in your trading to make it more efficient. If you can, pass this knowledge also to other traders and would-be traders. Go ahead and begin the movement that will sensitize people on the wonderful benefits of options trading.

Finally, if you found this book useful in any way, a review on Amazon is always appreciated!

www.ingramcontent.com/pod-product-compliance
Lightning Source LLC
Chambersburg PA
CBHW070342220526
45467CB00001B/217